Inside Science

Yoshinobu Nozaki
Kazuko Matsumoto
Alastair Graham-Marr

KINSEIDO

Kinseido Publishing Co., Ltd.
3-21 Kanda Jimbo-cho, Chiyoda-ku,
Tokyo 101-0051, Japan

Copyright © 2019 by Yoshinobu Nozaki
       Kazuko Matsumoto
       Alastair Graham-Marr

*All rights reserved. No part of this publication may
be reproduced, stored in a retrieval system, or transmitted,
in any form or by any means, electronic, mechanical,
photocopying, recording or otherwise, without the prior
permission of the publisher.*

First published 2019 by Kinseido Publishing Co., Ltd.

Cover design Takayuki Minegishi
Text design Shigoka Co., Ltd
Illustrations kamiharu

Material: Copyright © 2018 American Institute of Physics
  Inside Science is an editorially independent news service of the American Institute of Physics.

音声ファイル無料ダウンロード

http://www.kinsei-do.co.jp/download/4077

この教科書で 🎧 DL 00 の表示がある箇所の音声は、上記 URL または QR コードにて無料でダウンロードできます。自習用音声としてご活用ください。

▶ PC からのダウンロードをお勧めします。スマートフォンなどでダウンロードされる場合は、ダウンロード前に「解凍アプリ」をインストールしてください。
▶ URL は、検索ボックスではなくアドレスバー (URL 表示欄) に入力してください。
▶ お使いのネットワーク環境によっては、ダウンロードできない場合があります。

◎ CD 00 左記の表示がある箇所の音声は、教室用 CD (Class Audio CD) に収録されています。

はしがき

　本書は、米国の科学ニュースサイト Inside Science の映像を題材にした総合英語教材です。Inside Science は、米国物理学協会の運営のもと、正確であり且つ親しみやすい記事と映像を通じて最新の科学情報を発信し、高い人気を得ています。本書では、私たちを無理なく科学の世界へと導く映像付きの記事から 15 のトピックを厳選しました。これらのトピックは、「宇宙・天文」「エネルギー」「バイオミメティクス」「気象」「人工知能」など、科学の現在を映し出す内容をバランスよく含んでおり、理系・文系を問わず楽しめます。

　短い紹介文から始まる各ユニットは 6 ページ構成で、本文となる記事は内容理解のしやすさへの配慮から 2 つのパートに分割して編集しました。文中の単語に慣れるための Word-Exercise と、トピックに関連した語句を図・表やイラストから学ぶ Pre-Study でウォームアップをした後、映像を見ます。1st Watch は、最初に見た後の理解度を確認するエクササイズで、二種類の設問形式による内容把握問題を用意しました。

　視聴による全体像の把握を重視する 1st Watch に対して、細部の聴き取りへと力点を移したのが 2nd Watch です。スクリプトの、理解の鍵となる部分や数字、よく使われる語句などが空欄になっている部分を、映像または音声（映像とは違い、聞き取りやすく新録したものです）を聞いて埋める作業で、手ごたえを実感してください。空欄がすべて埋まったスクリプトは、優れたサイエンス系リーディング素材として活用が可能です。難解な用語や表現は含まれていませんが、スムーズな読解の手助けとして、末尾に Notes を添えました。

　2nd Watch の後に取り組む Vocabulary Build-Up と Phrase-Exercise は、文中に登場する重要単語と語句の運用力を高めるエクササイズです。必要に応じた語形変化が求められているので、文法の確認にも役立ちます。次の Composition-Exercise は、文中の重要表現や慣用表現の習得を目指す作文問題です。学習効果を高めるために、手を動かす作業が求められています。Summarizing-Exercise では、適語を補充して本文の要約を作ります。文章の構成力を養うとともに、本文を振り返り、内容の再確認を課すことで、エクササイズの締め括りとしました。

　こうしたエクササイズとは趣向を変え、ユニットとの関連性を保ちながら一息つける要素が盛り込まれているのが、最後の Stopover Dialogue です。男女二人が交わす、ユニットのトピックに関連した会話を聞いて質問に答える形式になっていますが、堅

苦しさはまったくありません。ユーモアとウィットに富むテンポの良い二人の会話は、楽しみながらユニットの学習を別の角度からとらえる機会を与えてくれるだけでなく、トピックへの関心をさらに深めてくれるでしょう。

　以上のように本書は、映像付き科学ニュースを学習教材として最大限に活用することを意図して作成されたテキストです。読者の英語力向上に役立つことを願うと同時に、ひとりでも多くの読者が、本書をきっかけに科学の世界の中―Inside Science―へと歩みを進めてゆくことも願っています。

　金星堂編集部の皆様には、多大なご協力と温かい励ましを常にいただきました。この場を借りてお礼を申し上げます。

編著者一同

Acknowledgements

The Original Sources Used in the Textbook

Unit 1   What If There Were No Moon?
                www.insidescience.org/video/what-would-happen-if-there-were-no-moon

Unit 2   The Physics of Fire
                www.insidescience.org/video/physics-fire

Unit 3   Shining A Light On Soils
                www.insidescience.org/video/shining-light-soils

Unit 4   Snowflake Photographer
                www.insidescience.org/video/snowflake-photographer

Unit 5   Two Severe Storms, Two Different Safety Directions
                www.insidescience.org/video/two-severe-storms-two-different-safety-directions

Unit 6   Love Highs and Lows
                www.insidescience.org/video/love-highs-and-lows

Unit 7   What Do Self-Driving Cars Really Need To Work Safely?
                www.insidescience.org/video/what-do-self-driving-cars-really-need-work-safely

Unit 8   Squid Parts Help Make Self-Healing Materials
                www.insidescience.org/video/squid-parts-help-make-self-healing-materials

Unit 9   Science Helps Squeeze Out Every Last Drop
                www.insidescience.org/video/science-helps-squeeze-out-every-last-drop

Unit 10   Detecting Fake Drugs
                www.insidescience.org/video/detecting-fake-drugs

Unit 11   The Touch And Feel Of Consumer Products
                www.insidescience.org/video/touch-and-feel-consumer-products

Unit 12   Tracking Space Trash
                www.insidescience.org/video/tracking-space-trash

Unit 13   Making Material Ready For Mars
                www.insidescience.org/video/making-materials-ready-mars

Unit 14   Bird's Secret To Soaring Super High
                www.insidescience.org/video/bird's-secret-soaring-super-high

Unit 15   Corn Kernels Could Make Better Biofuels
                www.insidescience.org/video/corn-kernels-could-make-better-biofuels

Contents

| Unit 1 | **No Moon at All?** [2分42秒] ─────── 6 |
月のない地球はいったいどうなる？

| Unit 2 | **Tackling Violent Wildfires** [2分51秒] ─────── 12 |
科学を武器に山火事と闘う

| Unit 3 | **Check the Soil First** [2分41秒] ─────── 18 |
適した土壌で生産高アップ

| Unit 4 | **The Beauty of Snowflakes** [2分30秒] ─────── 24 |
雪の結晶に魅せられた写真家

| Unit 5 | **Coping with the Extreme Weather** [2分46秒] ─────── 30 |
高度情報化社会における防災

| Unit 6 | **Is Love an Addiction?** [3分24秒] ─────── 36 |
恋愛をつかさどる脳の働き

| Unit 7 | **Self-Driving Future** [3分14秒] ─────── 42 |
未来に向けたハイテク搭載車両

| Unit 8 | **No Needle, No Thread?** [2分34秒] ─────── 48 |
自己修復する布の開発を目指して

Unit 9	**Aiming for a Perfect Squeeze** [2分42秒] ——— 54

ハスに学ぶムダのない生活

Unit 10	**Identifying Fake Drugs** [2分24秒] ——— 60

偽造薬を見破るアプリ

Unit 11	**Sensory Judgement is Important** [2分59秒] ——— 66

ヒット商品の鍵を握るサイコレオロジー

Unit 12	**Dangerous Debris in Space** [3分10秒] ——— 72

ゴミのない安全な宇宙空間を

Unit 13	**A Safer Mission to Mars** [3分06秒] ——— 78

火星の過酷なミッションを助ける新素材とは？

Unit 14	**Birds Know How to Glide** [3分09秒] ——— 84

鳥から学ぶムダなき究極の飛行術

Unit 15	**Better Biofuels from Corn** [3分23秒] ——— 90

新局面を迎えたバイオ燃料開発

Unit 1　No Moon at All?
月のない地球はいったいどうなる？

かぐや姫やうさぎの餅つきをはじめとする数々の伝説を生み出した月。月は、大昔から身近な天体として親しまれてきました。あまりにも身近であるために、夜空に月があるのは当たり前といった感覚になっていても不思議はありません。もしも月がなかったら、という仮定は、月が私たちの生活、ひいては存在に密接なかかわりをもつものであることを再認識させてくれます。

◉ Word-Exercise

次の単語の意味を下のa～eから選びましょう。

Part I
1. object [　]　2. Venus [　]　3. last [　]　4. sliver [　]　5. pull [　]

a. 続く　　b. 引力　　c. 細い一片　　d. 金星　　e. 物体

Part II
1. lunar [　]　2. block [　]　3. vary [　]　4. wild [　]　5. steady [　]

a. 変化する　　b. 荒れた　　c. 妨げる　　d. 月の　　e. 安定した

◉ Pre-Study

次の図は、月の満ち欠けを示したものです。指定された文字に続けて（　　）に適切な語を入れましょう。

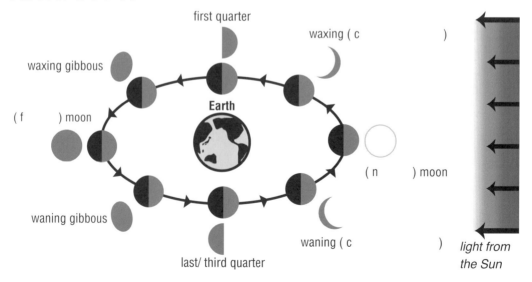

Unit 1 No Moon at All?

▶ 1st Watch

映像の Part I、II を観て、1 と 2 の英文が内容と一致していれば T を、していなければ F を ○ で囲みましょう。また、3 と 4 の英文が正しい内容を表すように破線部に入る適切な語（句）を a～c から選びましょう。

Part I ▶

1. Without the moon, the night sky would be fully lit up by Venus. [T / F]
2. If we had no moon, we could have over a thousand days in one year. [T / F]
3. A -------- is almost two thousand times brighter than Venus at its brightest.
    a. beacon
    b. full moon
    c. sliver of a nightlight
4. The gravitational force -------- the speed of the Earth's rotation.
    a. increases
    b. decreases
    c. measures

Part II ▶▶

1. On a moonless Earth, the size of the ocean tide would be always the same. [T / F]
2. No moon would lead to some very mild weather. [T / F]
3. Without the moon, --------.
    a. neither lunar nor solar eclipses would occur
    b. only lunar eclipses would occur
    c. only solar eclipses would occur
4. -------- is the cause of the seasons on our planet.
    a. The ocean tide
    b. The times Earth has evolved
    c. The Earth's tilt

▶ 2nd Watch

映像をもう一度観て、下線部に入る語句を記入して英文を完成させましょう。

Part I ▶ 　　　　　　　　　　　　　🎧 DL 02　💿 CD1-02

238,900 miles away, up in the sky…

Reporter: The moon, it can appear full, shining like a beacon in the night or just a sliver of a nightlight. Still, it's always there.

But what if we didn't have a moon?

Here's [1]_____
we would miss without it.

Nights would be much, much darker. The next brightest object in the night sky is Venus. But it still wouldn't be enough to light up the sky. A full moon is [2]_____

_____ than Venus is at its brightest.

But that's not the biggest difference you would notice. Without the moon, a day on Earth would only last six to twelve hours, meaning [3]_____

_____ in one year! That's because the Earth's rotation slows down over time thanks to the gravitational force, or pull of the moon, and without it, days [4]_____.

Part II ▶▶ 　　　　　　　　　　　　🎧 DL 03　💿 CD1-03

Reporter: A moonless Earth would also change the size of ocean tides, making them about [5]_____
_____ they are now. This means high tide would only come up this far and low tide would come up about this far.

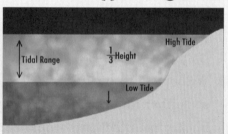

And just forget about seeing any lunar eclipses, or any solar eclipses. Without the moon, [6]_____
_____.

Without a moon, the tilt of our Earth's axis would vary over time. This could create some very wild weather. Right now, thanks to our moon, our axis stays tilted [7]_____. But without the moon the Earth might tilt too far over, or hardly tilt at all, leading to no seasons or even extreme seasons.

Without the moon helping to keep the Earth on a steady tilt, scientists have even imagined that [8]_____ at least the way it has.

So the next time you look up at the night sky, realize that the moon is making life here on Earth shine bright. This is Inside Science TV.

Notes
l.2 **beacon**（丘や塔などで燃やす信号用の）かがり火、灯台　l.24 **eclipses**（太陽・月の）食
l.26 **Earth's axis** 地軸

◉Vocabulary Build-Up

次のA，Bの（　）に、与えられた文字で始まる共通の単語を文中から探して記入し、文を完成させましょう（語形は必要に応じて変化させること）。

1. **A** The opportunity is too good to (**mi**　　　). I should take the chance of it.
   B I found some important papers were (**mi**　　　) from my desk.

2. **A** The ambulance was (**bl**　　　) by cars in the road.
   B The new building may (**bl**　　　) our view of the river.

3. **A** How long does the performance (**la**　　　)?
   B A balanced diet will have a long-(**la**　　　) impact on your health.

Phrase-Exercise

次の英文の（　）に適切な語句を語群から選びましょう（語形は必要に応じて変化させること）。

1. Hard work will (　　　　　　　) great success.

2. After many trials, the quality of the new item finally (　　　　　　　) to standard.

3. When I entered her room, she (　　　　　　　) at a ceiling holding back her tears.

look up　　light up　　come up　　lead to　　slow down

Composition-Exercise

[　] の語句を使い、日本文の意味を表す英文を完成させましょう。

1. 彼の演技のスコアは彼のライバルのスコアよりも4倍高い。[times]
   The score of his performance is _____
   his rival's score.

2. 彼女から返事がないので、私は彼女が私の電子メールを読んでいなかったのかもしれないと思った。[may]
   Not having heard from her, I imagined that _____
   _____ .

3. 地図がなければ、私たちが彼のオフィスに時間通りにたどり着くことはできなかっただろう。[manage]
   Without a map, we _____
   on time.

Summarizing-Exercise

以下は映像の要約です。(　　　) に与えられた文字で始まる適語を入れて、文を完成させましょう。

Just imagine if we didn't have the moon. The first thing you would notice is that the night sky would be much (**d**　　　). Secondly, each day would have a far shorter length. This is because the Earth would rotate more quickly when free from the (**p**　　　) of the moon. Without the moon's gravitational force, days would pass by in a (**b**　　　). Ocean tides would be affected on a moonless Earth. Furthermore, there would be no (**e**　　　), because no celestial body would (**b**　　　) the sun. Besides, the Earth's axis would vary over time, leading to extreme weather. Life on Earth may not have (**e**　　　) as we see now. Lastly, without romantic stories about the moon, life might be a little dull and lacking in imagination. Agreed?

Stopover Dialogue

月を題材にした映画を観た男女の短い会話を聞いて、以下の問題に答えましょう。

① 会話によれば、映画 *Galaxy Wars* の内容はどのようなものでしたか。

[　　　　　　　　　　　　　　　　　　　　　　　　　　　　　]

② 女性は月の引力がなければ、惑星 Uranium 7 がどうなると言っていますか。

[　　　　　　　　　　　　　　　　　　　　　　　　　　　　　]

③ 月を題材にした映画を3つ挙げてみましょう。

[　　　　　　　　　　　　　　　　　　　　　　　　　　　　　]

Unit 2 Tackling Violent Wildfires
科学を武器に山火事と闘う

近年、山火事は深刻な被害をもたらしながら世界各地で急増しています。予防の徹底と並んで注目されているのが延焼拡大化防止対策です。この対策の土台は、炎の性質に対する正確な知識と、山という地理的条件を考慮に入れた火災プロセスの解明です。ひとたび発生すると制御不能に陥り、人命を脅かす山火事に科学の力で対抗しようと多くの研究者が立ち上がっています。

Word-Exercise

次の単語の意味を下のa〜eから選びましょう。

Part I

1. ash [　] 2. unattended [　] 3. lightning [　] 4. property [　]
5. burnable [　]

| a. 灰 | b. 資産 | c. 稲妻 | d. 可燃の | e. 注意を払われていない |

Part II

1. creep [　] 2. process [　] 3. extreme [　] 4. tragic [　]
5. consequence [　]

| a. きわめて激しい | b. 悲劇的な | c. 過程 | d. 這う | e. 結果 |

Pre-Study

次の円グラフのA〜C、Eに入る自然災害を、Dを参考に、英語は下の語群から選び、それに相当する日本語を書き入れてみましょう。

Numbers of people affected by weather-related disasters in the world (1995-2015)

出典 UNISDER/CRED

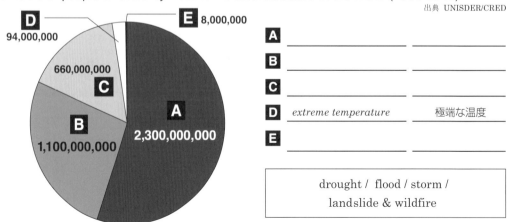

A _____ _____
B _____ _____
C _____ _____
D *extreme temperature*　極端な温度
E _____ _____

drought / flood / storm / landslide & wildfire

Unit 2 Tackling Violent Wildfires

1st Watch

映像の Part I、II を観て、1と2の英文が内容と一致していればTを、していなければFを○で囲みましょう。また、3と4の英文が正しい内容を表すように破線部に入る適切な語をa〜cから選びましょう。

Part I ▶

1. More than 90 percent of wildfires are caused by burning trash in the open-air fires. [T / F]
2. Some knowledge about the physics of fire is of great help to firefighters. [T / F]
3. Acres of forests can be -------- to ashes because of wildfires.
   a. controlled
   b. extinguished
   c. reduced
4. Basically, oxygen and fuel are -------- to start combustion.
   a. careless
   b. essential
   c. unattended

Part II ▶▶

1. In general, wildfires are likely to spread uphill. [T / F]
2. If winds blow downhill, then the fire can spread downhill, too. [T / F]
3. A -------- fire can spread in any direction.
   a. wind-dissipated
   b. wind-driven
   c. wind-released
4. Scientists are concerned about how greenhouse gas emissions are likely to make the wildfires more --------.
   a. costly
   b. extreme
   c. radiant

13

▶ 2nd Watch

映像をもう一度観て、下線部に入る語句を記入して英文を完成させましょう。

Part I　　　　　　　　　　　　　　　　🎧 DL 06　💿 CD1-06

Reporter: On average, about 8 million acres of land burns each year from wildfires. Big fires can reduce forests and grasslands to ash and can destroy homes and lives. Sadly, [1]_____ _____ wildland fires in the United States are caused by humans: carelessness, like unattended campfires, burning trash or waste, tossed-out cigarettes, and arson.

　The remaining 10 percent are usually started by lightning. [2]_____ _____ isn't easy. But knowing the science behind a burning blaze helps firefighters tackle the heat and flames to help save property, land and lives. Did you know wildfires often want to move uphill? It's all part of the physics of [3]_____.

Don Falk (the University of Arizona): The physics of combustion determine when and where we have a fire. Basically, in order to have combustion, you need fuel, something burnable; you need oxygen, which we're surrounded by; and then you need a source of energy to kick-start the combustion reaction. Now, 'the how' fires spread then is also [4]_____.

Part II　　　　　　　　　　　　　　　　🎧 DL 07　💿 CD1-07

Reporter: In general, fire will spread uphill. That's because fire, like the sun, releases radiant energy that [5]_____ _____. Some of the energy is dissipated into the sky. But the radiant energy that's released on the uphill side warms up nearby fuels, like grass and trees.

Falk: That means that those fuels are most likely to combust and the fire's going to creep uphill. So, the fire in effect actually pulls itself uphill by this process of preheating fuels and it's a [6]_____.

Reporter: For every 10 degrees of slope, a fire can double its speed.

Falk: Now, fires can ⁷_____, too. For example, in Southern California when we have the Santa Ana winds, those are often blowing downhill, and those fires can spread downhill very fast. Those are called wind-driven fires, and a wind-driven fire can spread in pretty much any direction.

Reporter: Many scientists think wildfires are likely to become more extreme as global temperatures continue to rise ⁸_____. They emphasize the importance of research to better reduce local risks from fires. Once a fire moves from wildlands into developed areas and neighborhoods, the flames can engulf homes and structures with tragic and costly consequences. This is Inside Science.

Notes

l.8 **tossed-out** 投げ捨てられた　*l.9* **arson** 放火　*l.12* **blaze**（比較的大きく燃えさかる）炎（flame〈ろうそくの炎のように舌を思わせる炎〉よりも勢いが強い）　*l.15* **combustion** 燃焼　*l.16* **fuel** 燃料　*l.18* **kick-start ~** ~を始動させる　*l.31* **For every 10 degrees of slope** 10度の勾配につき　*l.33* **Santa Ana winds** サンタアナの風（カリフォルニア州において、内陸部に広がる砂漠から沿岸部に向かって吹く、乾燥した高温の局地風）　*l.41* **engulf** 飲みこむ

Vocabulary Build-Up

次のA, Bの（　）に、与えられた文字で始まる共通の単語を文中から探して記入し、文を完成させましょう（語形は必要に応じて変化させること）。

1. **A** I enjoyed the view of Tokyo and its (**su**　　　) areas from the Tokyo Skytree.
   B The Prime Minister quickly moved to the car (**su**　　　) by some bodyguards.

2. **A** Our tent was almost (**bl**　　　) away by a strong wind.
   B We walked against strong winds (**bl**　　　) through the tall buildings.

3. **A** Prices have (**ri**　　　) by 10% this year.
   B The film director was pleased with the (**ri**　　　) reputation of his works.

Phrase-Exercise

次の英文の（　　）に適切な語句を語群から選びましょう（語形は必要に応じて変化させること）。

1. Can you make tea while I (　　　　　　) the pizza in the microwave?

2. He was so busy that he (　　　　　　) his junk mail without opening it.

3. We opened the windows and the smell of gas finally (　　　　　　) the air.

| cause by | dissipate into | heat up | toss out | reduce to |

Composition-Exercise

[　] の語句を使い、日本文の意味を表す英文を完成させましょう。

1. 地滑りの速度は、傾斜の角度が10度増すごとに、ほぼ倍化する。[double]
   A landslide can roughly _____
   for every added 10-degree angle.

2. 新聞各紙によれば、首相は健康状態を理由に辞職するそうだ。[likely, due]
   According to some newspapers, the Prime Minister _____
   _____ his health condition.

3. 消防士たちが、もし火災がどう広がるかを知れば、それは彼らが私たちの生命と財産を守る手助けになる。[how, spreads]
   If firefighters _____,
   it will help them save our lives and property.

Summarizing-Exercise

以下は映像の要約です。(　　　) に与えられた文字で始まる適語を入れて、文を完成させましょう。

> Every year, some 8 million acres of land are reduced to ashes. To conquer these devastating wildfires, we need to understand the scientific nature of fire. Basically, the (**p**　　　) of fire would show us that fuel, (**o**　　　), and a source of energy are necessary to start a fire. In addition to these facts, we need to take notice of "how" the fire actually (**s**　　　). Such knowledge will be of really practical help to firefighters. As a matter of fact, fire (**s**　　　) uphill. This is because heat, or radiant (**e**　　　), from combustion, creeps uphill and warms the surrounding vegetation, making it ready to (**b**　　　). Another factor is wind, which can drive the fire downhill, or, in fact, in any (**d**　　　). Today, scientists fear wildfires will become more (**e**　　　) as a result of global warming, threatening to endanger more human life.

Stopover Dialogue

火事に関する男女の短い会話を聞いて、以下の問題に答えましょう。

① 「火除地（ひよけち）」は、誰がいつ設置を命令しましたか。

[　　　　　　　　　　　　　　　　　　　　　　　]

② 火除地は本来の目的とは別に、どんなことに使われていましたか。

[　　　　　　　　　　　　　　　　　　　　　　　]

③ 火除地をつくるきっかけとなった大火事について調べ、名称・発生年・その後の影響を記入してみましょう。

[　　　　　　　　　　　　　　　　　　　　　　　]

Unit 3 Check the Soil First
適した土壌で生産高アップ

分光学を土壌組成の分析に援用した研究が進行中です。土壌に最適な作物を栽培することは、環境への配慮に欠けた農作を食い止めるとともに、農業労働者が払ってきた無駄な労力とコストの削減にもつながります。作物の生産性の向上のみならず、農業労働者の生活水準向上も視野に入れたこの研究の原動力は、農地も農民も疲弊しきった開発途上国の過酷な現状の改善を目指す研究者の熱意です。

Word-Exercise

次の単語の意味を下のa〜eから選びましょう。

Part I
1. chemical [　]　2. fertilizer [　]　3. crop [　]　4. additional [　]
5. livelihood [　]

| a. 暮らし | b. 作物 | c. 肥料 | d. 化学の | e. 付加的な |

Part II
1. deforestation [　]　2. sustainably [　]　3. reliably [　]　4. element [　]
5. overall [　]

| a. 元素 | b. 全体の | c. 森林伐採 | d. 持続的に | e. 確実に |

Pre-Study

次の円グラフは大気の組成を示したものです。空欄に入る適切な気体を、与えられた文字で始まるように記入しましょう。

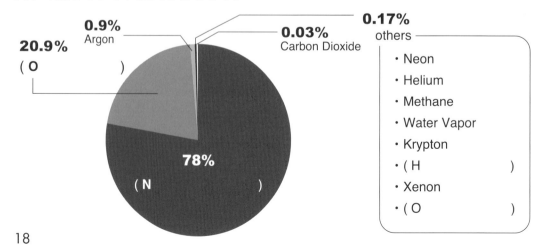

1st Watch

映像の Part I、II を観て、1 と 2 の英文が内容と一致していれば T を、していなければ F を○で囲みましょう。また、3 と 4 の英文が正しい内容を表すように破線部に入る適切な語（句）を a～c から選びましょう。

Part I

1. Optical technology enables us to understand the chemical composition of various materials. [T / F]
2. Crop yields can be improved dramatically by using fertilizers that the government recommends. [T / F]
3. Fertilizers don't necessarily work as they are -------- to.
   a. expected
   b. improved
   c. taken
4. Aided by these much lower cost devices, productivity could be --------.
   a. boosted greatly
   b. made less acidic
   c. sold at low prices

Part II

1. Basically, the practice of deforestation will make the soil very rich in nutrients. [T / F]
2. In places where people depend on agriculture for their living, better crops are of major importance. [T / F]
3. Scientists try to help farmers in sub-Saharan Africa to achieve -------- agriculture.
   a. additional   b. primitive   c. sustainable
4. In order to decide on an optimal fertilizer, farmers should take into account information about --------.
   a. how to improve their incomes from agriculture
   b. the historical weather patterns as well as the soil conditions
   c. what fertilizer the local government recommends

▶ 2nd Watch

映像をもう一度観て、下線部に入る語句を記入して英文を完成させましょう。

Part I ▶   DL 10   CD1-10

Matt Keller (a research scientist at Intellectual Ventures Laboratory): We're working on various applications of spectroscopy in low resource settings. So, what that means is using optical technology to really understand the chemical makeup of different materials.

Reporter: One material Keller looks at is soil—soil that farmers [1]_____ _____, to feed families, and sell at markets. Soil composition is important for producing bumper crops year after year.

Keller: The idea here is when [2]_____ _____—so, they know, you know, nitrogen, phosphorous, carbon, pH and all of those good things—then they can get dramatic improvements in their, in their crop yields by using the right kind of fertilizer that's matched exactly to their soil.

Reporter: It turns out that fertilizers [3]_____ _____ to help improve crops.

Keller: For example, one of the fertilizers that has been recommended by governments over the years, without knowing what the soil is like, uh, actually has been making certain soils very acidic to the point where, you know, additional fertilizer doesn't help because the soil is too acidic.

So, the idea here is by bringing the testing to farmers [4]_____ _____, then the productivity by small farmers can be boosted and they can improve their incomes and therefore their livelihoods.

Part II ▶   DL 11   CD1-11

Reporter: When farmers in places like sub-Saharan Africa cannot grow enough food, [5]_____ _____ or using land not suited for crops. The result has been problems with soil erosion and poor nutrients within soil. Keller wants to help them [6]

Unit 3 Check the Soil First

Keller: We can basically input the spectral data, which can tell you, you know, how much of the certain elements or what the other physical properties are of the soil and then merge that up with information about maybe ⁷_____, information about what local crops work well in different soil conditions, and then the overall outcome then is okay, so what is the optimal treatment in terms of fertilizer. What is the best plant to put here?

Reporter: The work Keller does could be instrumental in helping farmers grow better crops, especially in places where most of the population ⁸_____.

Keller: But getting, you know, crops to grow to, you know, to feed your family and provide income is extremely important. I mean it's absolutely critical for their lives.

Reporter: This is Inside Science.

Notes
l.3 **spectroscopy** 分光学 *l.5* **optical technology** 光学技術 *l.6* **chemical makeup** 化学組成
l.12 **nitrogen** 窒素 *l.12* **phosphorous** リン *l.14* **crop yields** 生産量 *l.23* **be boosted** 上昇する
l.30 **erosion** 浸食 *l.33* **spectral data** スペクトルデータ（スペクトル：光や電磁波を分光器によって波長順に分解し、波長順に並べたもの） *l.34* **physical properties** 物理的特性 *l.35* **merge** 組み合わせる

◉ Vocabulary Build-Up

次のA, Bの（　）に、与えられた文字で始まる共通の単語を文中から探して記入し、文を完成させましょう（語形は必要に応じて変化させること）。

1. **A** Sweets flavored with *matcha* always (**se**   ) well to foreign tourists.
   B The sales clerk emphasized the (**se**   ) points of the new product.

2. **A** He was (**br**   ) up in a large family.
   B Could you (**br**   ) me another cup of coffee, please?

3. **A** Every meal is (**pr**   ) in my dormitory, so I don't need to pay.
   B Newspapers are responsible for (**pr**   ) accurate information.

Phrase-Exercise

次の英文の（　）に適切な語句を語群から選びましょう（語形は必要に応じて変化させること）。

1. After a heated discussion, it (　　　　　　　) that his hypothesis was wrong.

2. The director has been (　　　　　　　) a new film for a decade.

3. With a successful career as a chemist, he is well (　　　　　　　) leading our lab.

work on　　turn out　　resort to　　suit for　　depend on

Composition-Exercise

[　] の語句を使い、日本文の意味を表す英文を完成させましょう。

1. 山頂の天気の様子がわからないまま、彼らは登山を始めた。[what, like]
They started to climb without _____
near the top of the mountain.

2. 天気が悪いと、建設工事はつねに予定通りには進むとは限らない。[always, as]
If the weather is bad, construction work doesn't _____
_____.

3. 我々の新しい研究室は、エイズや白血病などの死に至る多くの病気の治療法の発見に貢献するだろう。[instrumental in]
Our new laboratory _____
for many lethal diseases such as AIDS and leukemia.

Summarizing-Exercise

以下は映像の要約です。(　　　) に与えられた文字で始まる適語を入れて、文を完成させましょう。

> For all the farmers, it is of prime importance to grow bumper crops constantly. One essential way to (**i**　　　) cultivation is through the appropriate use of (**f**　　　), which helps the soil work effectively to yield better crops. Needless to say, first of all, farmers must understand the quality of their soil. If the soil gets too (**a**　　　), for example, it will often lead to a poor harvest. Now scientists are introducing spectroscopic devices that can test the soil and show the farmers exactly what ingredients their soil contains. If they know the precise quantity of, say, nitrogen or (**c**　　　), in the soil, the farmers will be able to use the right kinds of fertilizer that will (**m**　　　) their soil. Then greater and better crops can be expected. So, such low-cost technology may aid the realization of (**s**　　　) agriculture.

Stopover Dialogue

トマトに関する男女の短い会話を聞いて、以下の問題に答えましょう。

① 女性が毎日トマトを食べる理由は何ですか。

［　　　　　　　　　　　　　　　　　　　　　　　　　　　］

② 女性が特にメキシコ産のトマトが好きなのはなぜですか。

［　　　　　　　　　　　　　　　　　　　　　　　　　　　］

③ 会話の最後に登場するユカタン半島の巨大隕石跡について調べ、名称や規模、発見の経緯を書いてみましょう。

［　　　　　　　　　　　　　　　　　　　　　　　　　　　］

Unit 4 The Beauty of Snowflakes
雪の結晶に魅せられた写真家

「雪は天から送られてきた手紙である」―研究対象の雪に対する深い思い入れを伝えるこの言葉を残した中谷宇吉郎博士が生まれた頃、雪に魅了され、結晶の撮影に没頭したアメリカ人農夫がいました。約5千枚に及ぶ彼の写真は、現在、高い学術的評価を受けています。酷寒の中、種々の工夫を凝らした手作りの道具で結晶を撮り続けた人物の物語です。

Word-Exercise

次の単語の意味を下のa～eから選びましょう。

Part I ▶

1. fragile [   ] 2. individual [   ] 3. trade [   ] 4. vision [   ] 5. detailed [   ]

| a. 職業 | b. 個々の | c. 壊れやすい | d. 視覚 | e. 緻密な |

Part II ▶▶

1. microscope [   ] 2. tough [   ] 3. broom [   ] 4. knob [   ] 5. legacy [   ]

| a. 過酷な | b. （器具の）つまみ | c. 顕微鏡 | d. 遺産 | e. ほうき |

Pre-Study

雪の結晶は基本的に六角形（hexagon）ですが、それ以外の以下の図形について名称を英語で書いてみましょう。

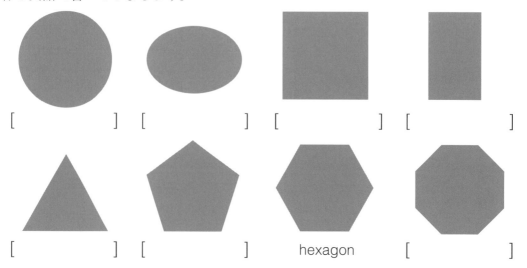

[   ] [   ] [   ] [   ]

[   ] [   ] hexagon [   ]

Unit 4　The Beauty of Snowflakes

▶ 1st Watch

映像の Part I、II を観て、1と2の英文が内容と一致していれば T を、していなければ F を○で囲みましょう。また、3と4の英文が正しい内容を表すように破線部に入る適切な語（句）を a〜c から選びましょう。

Part I ▶

1. As snowflakes are very delicate, you must be careful when taking a picture of them.　　　　[T / F]
2. Wilson Bentley made a living by working as a scientist.　　　　[T / F]
3. The difficulty of photographing snowflakes never -------- Bentley from challenging himself to do it.
   a. faced
   b. imagined
   c. prevented
4. Bentley's photomicrographs were detailed pictures that -------- the actions of snowflakes.
   a. fell
   b. froze
   c. stood

Part II ▶▶

1. By connecting a camera to a microscope, Bentley obtained snowflake pictures in close-up.　　　　[T / F]
2. It was too cold in his unheated woodshed to work the camera properly.　　　　[T / F]
3. Bentley took lots of photomicrographs under -------- conditions.
   a. crystal
   b. fast
   c. tough
4. Modern camera technology enables you to -------- snowflakes in motion.
   a. collect
   b. scan
   c. track

25

▶ 2nd Watch

映像をもう一度観て、下線部に入る語句を記入して英文を完成させましょう。

Part I ▶   🎧 DL 14   ◎ CD1-14

Reporter: Snowflakes. They are beautiful and fragile, and also very difficult to photograph. But that didn't stop one scientist from trying.

5 **Reporter:** Can you imagine how hard it would be to photograph a teeny-tiny, individual snowflake crystal? Then imagine the challenges that Wilson Bentley faced back [1]_____.

10 **Terry Nathan (an atmospheric scientist at the University of California at Davis):** Wilson Bentley pioneered in photographing snow crystals, snowflakes and raindrops. He was [2]_____. When snowflakes are falling by the billions from clouds, through photography, we can freeze that motion, understand how fast it's falling, how those snowflakes might 15 be connected to the cloud itself and the nature of the storm. Photography allows us to see things that are [3]_____.

Reporter: Bentley took what are called photomicrographs that were detailed pictures of snow crystals.

Part II ▶   🎧 DL 15   ◎ CD1-15

Nathan: A photomicrograph is simply 20 [4]_____ so that you can get very detailed, close-up pictures. Now, with Wilson Bentley, there were challenges. He worked under very tough conditions. It 25 was cold. It was snowing. He had to collect these snow crystals on a little black board, take them into his unheated woodshed to photograph.

He [5]_____ from the board to the microscope slide, which is a very delicate process, and used a little, initially 30 little, uh, sliver from a broom, his mother's broom to get that onto the slide, he even had to kind of jury-rig a focusing knob, a string running to the microscope 'cause he couldn't reach it, so he turned this little knob, and he used that mostly throughout his whole life.

Reporter: Bentley's work led to better camera technology like the multi-angle snowflake camera, which tracks ^{6}_____

_____ and the fast-line scanning camera, which measures the two-dimensional shape of raindrops.

Nathan: But He made over 5,000 photomicrographs over 46 years, and ^{7}_____ _____, the Smithsonian and other places.

Reporter: A man ahead of his time left a legacy for science in snowflake photos that ^{8}_____ anytime soon. This is Inside Science.

Notes
l.6 **teeny-tiny** 小さな *l.17* **photomicrographs** 顕微鏡写真 *l.27* **woodshed** まき小屋 *l.31* **jury-rig** 間に合わせの物を作る *l.38* **fast-line** 高速の *l.39* **two-dimensional** 二次元の *l.42* **the Smithsonian** スミソニアン協会（ワシントン D.C. にある、国立の学術機関。19の博物館、研究施設から構成される）

◉Vocabulary Build-Up

次の A, B の（　）に、与えられた文字で始まる共通の単語を文中から探して記入し、文を完成させましょう（語形は必要に応じて変化させること）。

1. **A** My laptop is (**fr**　　　) now so I can't send you the file.
   B We put some (**fr**　　　) meat on a microwave-safe plate.

2. **A** Our project (**fa**　　　) a critical shortage of funds last year.
   B I'd like to reserve a single room (**fa**　　　) the ocean.

3. **A** Our boss will be (**tr**　　　) to the Osaka branch as of April 1.
   B Let me (**tr**　　　) your call to our manager. He is the right person to speak to about it.

📍Phrase-Exercise

次の英文の（　　）に適切な語句を語群から選びましょう（語形は必要に応じて変化させること）。

1. I finally realized the trouble was because my laptop wasn't (　　　　　　　　) the internet.

2. No one disagrees that he (　　　　　　　　) inventing a modern railway system.

3. The snow has (　　　　　　　　) when the sun came out.

fall from　　lead to　　melt away　　connect to　　pioneer in

📍Composition-Exercise

[　]の語句を使い、日本文の意味を表す英文を完成させましょう。

1. 超低周波音センサーは人間の通常の聴覚レベルを超える低音の検出を可能にさせる。[allow]
Infrasound sensors _____
beyond the normal limit of human hearing.

2. 冬の海で泳ぐのがどれほど寒いか想像できますか。[how, would]
Can you imagine _____
_____ in winter's ocean?

3. 誰でも無重力を体験できるように、その施設の入場は無料になっている。[so that]
Admission into the facility is free _____
_____.

Unit 4 The Beauty of Snowflakes

Summarizing-Exercise

DL 16 CD1-16

以下は映像の要約です。(　　　)に与えられた文字で始まる適語を入れて、文を完成させましょう。

Back in the 1800s, Wilson Bentley first started to photograph snowflakes. He was a farmer by (t　　　), but stirred by scientific passion, he continued the hard job in his cold woodshed and, ultimately, over a period of 40 years made more than 5000 pictures of tiny figures of snow (c　　　). These pictures had exquisite beauty of their own, but also were useful for understanding more about the actual conditions of the atmosphere. To make a photomicrograph —a delicate close-up picture—he had to (c　　　) a camera to a microscope and using a sliver from a broom, put the snowflake on to the (s　　　) with utmost care. Also he had to create a (f　　　) knob of his own. Indeed, he was a pioneer in microphotography, and his (l　　　) lives on in the more advanced technology of today, such as the multi-angle snowflake camera.

Stopover Dialogue

DL 17

研究室での男女の短い会話を聞いて、以下の問題に答えましょう。

① 男性はなぜお腹をすかせていたのですか。

[　　　　　　　　　　　　　　　　　　　　　　　　]

② 男性が見ていた碁石のようなものの正体は何でしたか？

[　　　　　　　　　　　　　　　　　　　　　　　　]

③ 会話の最後で②の回答がレンズの語源であることがわかりましたが、では有名なカメラメーカーのキャノンとミノルタ（現・コニカミノルタ）の語源について調べてみましょう。

[　　　　　　　　　　　　　　　　　　　　　　　　]

Unit 5　Coping with the Extreme Weather

高度情報化社会における防災

近年、異なる種類の自然災害の同時発生率が急増する中、的確な避難や迅速な救護活動を行う目的で気象研究者と社会科学者が連携を始めました。情報を前にした時の人々の反応や行動に関する社会科学者の知見は、優れたテクノロジーを駆使して分析された気象情報の効果的かつ適切な伝達に威力を発揮することが期待されます。その伝達で重要な役割を果たすのが SNS です。

◯ Word-Exercise

次の単語の意味を下の a～e から選びましょう。

Part I ▶

1. contradict [　]　2. meteorologist [　]　3. threat [　]　4. viewer [　]
5. sturdy [　]

　　　　a. 頑丈な　　b. 気象学者　　c. 脅威　　d. 相反する　　e. 視聴者

Part II ▶▶

1. structure [　]　2. excessive [　]　3. atmosphere [　]　4. complex [　]
5. compelling [　]

　　　　a. 複雑な　　b. 大気　　c. 過度の　　d. 建造物　　e. 切実な

◯ Pre-Study

次は風の強さを 0～12 に分類したビューフォート風力階級（Beaufort scale）です。以下の A～E の空所に入る語を語群から選んで記入しましょう。

語群　(gale　storm　breeze　air　hurricane)

Force	Description	Wind Speed	Conditions
0	Calm	1 km/h	Smoke rises vertically.
1	Light (A)	1.1~5.5 km/h	Smoke drift indicates wind direction.
2	Light (B)	5.6~11 km/h	Wind felt on face, leaves rustle.
3	Gentle (B)	12~19 km/h	Leaves constantly moving, light flags extended.
4	Moderate (B)	20~28 km/h	Dust, leaves lifted, small tree branches move.
5	Fresh (B)	29~38 km/h	Small trees in leaf begin to sway.
6	Strong (B)	39~49 km/h	Larger tree branches moving, whistling in wires.
7	Moderate (C)	50~61 km/h	Whole trees moving, hard to walk against wind.
8	Fresh (C)	62~74 km/h	Twigs breaking off trees, hard to step forward.
9	Strong (C)	75~88 km/h	Slight structural damage occurs.
10	Whole (C)	89~102 km/h	Serious structural damage. Trees broken or uprooted.
11	(D)	103~117 km/h	Exceptionally high waves, foam patches cover sea.
12	(E) force	118+ km/h	Sea completely white with driving spray.

Unit 5 Coping with the Extreme Weather

▶ 1st Watch

映像の Part I、II を観て、1と2の英文が内容と一致していればTを、していなければFを○で囲みましょう。また、3と4の英文が正しい内容を表すように破線部に入る適切な語（句）をa～cから選びましょう。

Part I ▶

1. Two severe weather events won't occur together at the same time. [T / F]
2. Instructions for surviving a tornado may conflict with those for a flash flood. [T / F]
3. "TORFF" refers to a weather event in which --------.
   a. a flash flood triggers a tornado
   b. a tornado happens followed by a flash flood
   c. a tornado and a flash flood occur simultaneously
4. You should seek your shelter -------- during a tornado outbreak.
   a. in a weather service office
   b. in the highest place in your house
   c. underground

Part II ▶▶

1. The atmosphere is so complex that it is often hard to release correct weather warnings in advance. [T / F]
2. Information on a tornado must be communicated to the public immediately, as its threat is the most urgent. [T / F]
3. It is a complex job to -------- down every aspect of the atmosphere when giving a weather forecast.
   a. pick
   b. nail
   c. share
4. Both physical and social sciences can cooperate with each other in order to --------.
   a. create safe places for the public
   b. identify which forecast is accurate
   c. offer correct instructions quickly

31

▶ 2nd Watch

映像をもう一度観て、下線部に入る語句を記入して英文を完成させましょう。

Part I ▶   🎧 DL 18 💿 CD1-18

Reporter: Tornadoes and flash floods can ¹_____. But the safety instructions for what you're supposed to do during each one often contradict one another.

Now meteorologists and social scientists are working together to identify when these two severe weather events occur together and how best to communicate that information to the public.

Reporter: Tornadoes and flash flooding are two separate severe weather events. But ²_____, they can occur at the same time.

Jennifer Henderson, PhD (the University of Colorado): TORFF is tornado plus flash floods, and it's when there are two threats that exist at the same time in the same space, or at least the warnings do.

Reporter: But the safety information that viewers receive from their local national weather service office or broadcast meteorologists during these two severe weather events can be conflicting. For tornadoes, you should seek safety in a sturdy structure or underground. But if a flash flood is coming, the last place you want to be is where fast-moving water ³_____.

Part II ▶   🎧 DL 19 💿 CD1-19

Erik Nielsen, PhD candidate (Colorado State University): For tornadoes, you're supposed to go to the lowest central room of your home, structure, or wherever you might be, but for flash flood, you're supposed to ⁴_____.

And so, if you're under both threats at the same time, you could potentially pick incorrectly and put yourself in excessive danger.

So the thing that I think I've learned is that the atmosphere is extremely

complex, that we, as meteorologists, every day⁵ _____
_____ as best we can. But it is so unbelievably complex to really
nail down everything in enough time in advance to⁶ _____
_____ to warn the people.

Henderson: One of the, the newer ways that the forecasters are communicating these threats is⁷ _____. And so, there are researchers in the social science community who are trying to understand what kinds of information people on social media are picking up—what is it that you most respond to, what is it that you share the most often, and what's the most compelling in terms of making you want to take some sort of action, whether it's share the information or seek more information or take some sort of action.

Reporter: While Henderson and Nielsen continue to study the physical and social science of tornado and flash flood events, their goal remains to identify severe weather threats⁸ _____, and communicate that information quickly to the public. This is Inside Science.

Notes
l.1 **tornadoes** トルネード（アメリカ中西部で発生する局地的な巨大竜巻のこと）　*l.10* **weather events** 気象事象
l.29 **potentially** 潜在的に、もしかすると

◉ Vocabulary Build-Up

次のA，Bの（　）に、与えられた文字で始まる共通の単語を文中から探して記入し、文を完成させましょう（語形は必要に応じて変化させること）。

1. **A** The newly discovered insects have yet to be (**id**   ).
   B We need to (**id**   ) some possible problems for our new research program.

2. **A** The repeated misunderstandings have (**th**   ) their good relationships.
   B Too much stress may cause you life-(**th**   ) diseases.

3. **A** The politician smiled a little and (**re**   ) calm despite the booing.
   B The mountain is still covered with some (**re**   ) snow.

Phrase-Exercise

次の英文の（　）に適切な語句を語群から選びましょう（語形は必要に応じて変化させること）。

1. Could you (   ) a liter of milk from the supermarket on your way back home?

2. I have to (   ) to my colleagues that our boss will be transferred soon.

3. (   ) the cheers of the audience, the pianist played an encore piece.

> get the word out   nail down   try to   respond to   pick up

Composition-Exercise

[　] の語句を使い、日本文の意味を表す英文を完成させましょう。

1. 安全性に関して最も緊急なことについて、あなたがたと議論したい。[what's, terms]
I'd like to have a discussion with you about _____
_____ of safety.

2. 行方不明の鍵が、まさかここで見つかるとは思わなかった。[last, expected]
This is the _____
the missing key.

3. ホテルコンシェルジュとして、彼はできる限り最上のサービスをゲストに提供すべく懸命に努力している。[hard, provide]
As a hotel concierge, he _____
the guest as best he can.

Summarizing-Exercise 　DL 20　CD1-20

以下は映像の要約です。(　　　) に与えられた文字で始まる適語を入れて、文を完成させましょう。

A (f　　　) flood is a sudden rush of water caused by heavy rain. Another natural disaster that is happening more and more frequently today is tornadoes. What if both violent events (o　　　) at the same time? When a tornado is approaching, you are advised to seek (s　　　) in the basement. However, if a (f　　　) flood is also happening, the underground may be flooded with water. On the contrary, at the very moment you moved up to some higher place in the house in order to avoid the incoming (f　　　) flood, you may unexpectedly be informed of an oncoming tornado. Then, the upper floor is the most dangerous place as it is vulnerable to the (s　　　) tornado. Of course two separate warnings must not conflict with each other. So, once a flash flood and a tornado happen together, a (w　　　) based on accurate information must be released as soon as (p　　　) through the most easily accessible media—social media, for example.

Stopover Dialogue　　DL 21　CD1-21

迫り来る自然災害に関する男女の短い会話を聞いて、以下の問題に答えましょう。

① 2人はなぜ地下に避難できないのですか。

[　　　　　　　　　　　　　　　　　　　　　　　　　　]

② 結局、2人はどこへ避難すると考えられますか。

[　　　　　　　　　　　　　　　　　　　　　　　　　　]

③ あなたが住む地域の竜巻や洪水が起きたときの対策（避難経路等）について調べ、わかったことを記入してみましょう。

[　　　　　　　　　　　　　　　　　　　　　　　　　　]

Unit 6   Is Love an Addiction?
恋愛をつかさどる脳の働き

「恋煩い」「恋は麻疹のようなもの」といいますが、現代医学は恋愛中の脳と麻薬依存患者の脳の酷似をつきとめ、恋愛と病いの相関関係を実証しました。各種依存症対策として快楽を求める脳のメカニズム解明が進む中、従来、心や精神の問題といわれた恋愛が、科学の側面からも語られ始めています。恋愛攻略本に脳の話が載るようになった近年の傾向は、そのひとつの現れといえます。

Word-Exercise

次の単語の意味を下のa～eから選びましょう。

Part I ▶

1. obsessive [　]　2. addictive [　]　3. progression [　]　4. tolerance [　]
5. drive [　]

| a. 駆り立てる　b. 中毒性の　c. 進行過程　d. 耐性　e. 憑りつかれたような |

Part II ▶▶

1. intimacy [　]　2. stimulate [　]　3. specific [　]　4. active [　]
5. ingredient [　]

| a. 刺激する　b. 特定の　c. 親密さ　d. 成分　e. 活性化する |

Pre-Study

空所に入る適切な単語を下の語群から選び、感情を表す単語のグループ分けを完成させましょう。

語群
amazed　brokenhearted
mad　uneasy
anxious　delighted
furious　astonished
pleased　depressed

Unit 6 Is Love an Addiction?

▶ 1st Watch

映像の Part I、II を観て、1と2の英文が内容と一致していればTを、していなければFを○で囲みましょう。また、3と4の英文が正しい内容を表すように破線部に入る適切な語（句）をa〜cから選びましょう。

Part I ▶

1. A cocaine addict gradually develops a tolerance for the drug as time goes on. [T / F]
2. The reward system works when you experience pleasant things. [T / F]
3. The chemical dopamine sends out -------- that something joyful is happening to you.
    a. an addiction
    b. a brain
    c. a signal
4. When the effect of a drug --------, the addict will crave more doses of it.
    a. builds up
    b. breaks up
    c. wears off

Part II ▶▶

1. Physical contact between a man and a woman will directly stimulate the reward pathways in their brains. [T / F]
2. When you are disappointed in love, serotonin helps you lose interest. [T / F]
3. Love will let the brain release the chemicals, such as oxytocin or serotonin, which -------- the reward system.
    a. stimulate
    b. stress
    c. support
4. Oxytocin, which spurred your love, can also cure you of --------.
    a. a silver lining
    b. broken-hearted disappointment
    c. the supersized love storm

▶ 2nd Watch

映像をもう一度観て、下線部に入る語句を記入して英文を完成させましょう。

Part I ▶   DL 22 CD1-22

Alistair Jennings, PhD, neuroscientist: Love can make us joyful, obsessive, sometimes sick. And addictive drugs do, well, the same. But [1]_____ _____?

Love and addictive drugs share the same progression. The initial, euphoric, honeymoon period; a drawn-out stage of constant usage, gradually building up a tolerance; and finally the break-up and going cold-turkey. But why would your brain treat your lover like a line of cocaine?

Your brain has a system for rewarding you for [2]_____ _____. It's a network of areas of your simpler midbrain and your more complicated frontal lobes. The reward system communicates via the chemical dopamine. Dopamine is released to signal to the rest of the brain that something good has happened to you.

[3]_____. They turbocharge the feeling of reward, but when they wear off, you're left craving another dopamine hit. [4]_____. And different drugs drive the reward system in different ways; some directly, some through the release of chemicals like serotonin, oxytocin, and opioids. But love hits all of those pathways at the same time.

Part II ▶   DL 23 CD1-23

Jennings: Social contact, physical intimacy, and the promise of sex all directly stimulate an increase in dopamine.

[5]_____ _____, hugging, and orgasm release oxytocin from the hypothalamus, which indirectly stimulates the reward pathway and it makes those rewarding feelings [6]_____, special person.

Love also releases serotonin and opioids, the active ingredient in heroin! It's a

38

perfect storm. And by the end of it, you are completely addicted to someone, rather than something. So it's no wonder that when you finally fall out of love, and all those chemicals stop coursing round your system, the comedown can be hard. And ⁷_____, now is when your brain starts releasing stress hormones that can make you sick, and make you crave what you've lost.

But there is a silver lining. Oxytocin—the same chemical that supersized the love storm—is here to help. Oxytocin is also ⁸_____ _____ with your friends and people that you care about, which is why support from your friends, and from other groups, has been shown to help recovering addicts, and maybe broken-hearted exes.

For Inside Science TV, I'm Ali Jennings. Thanks for watching.

Notes
l.1 **neuroscientist** 神経科学者 *l.7* **euphoric** 興奮状態の *l.8* **drawn-out** 長引く *l.9* **go cold-turkey** 禁断症状になる *l.10* **a line of cocaine** 一服のコカイン（コカインを鼻から吸引する時に、テーブルや紙の上に出した粉末を剃刀の刃やカードなどで細い線上に時に形を整えることに由来する表現） *l.13* **frontal lobes** 前頭葉 *l.17* **left craving** 渇望状態におかれる *l.20* **serotonin** セロトニン（脳内神経伝達物質） *l.20* **oxytocin** オキシトシン（ドーパミン、セロトニンの分泌を促進するホルモン） *l.20* **opioids** オピオイド（麻酔性鎮痛剤） *l.27* **hypothalamus** 視床下部 *l.38* **silver lining** 希望の兆し

♥Vocabulary Build-Up

次のA，Bの（　）に、与えられた文字で始まる共通の単語を文中から探して記入し、文を完成させましょう（語形は必要に応じて変化させること）。

1. **A** Many couples try hard to (**sh**　　　) the housework.
   B I don't mind (**sh**　　　) the table with other people.

2. **A** We (**hu**　　　) each other and said goodbye at the airport.
   B The winners are (**hu**　　　) and clapping each other on the back.

3. **A** Five years of training in the gym made him a strongly (**bu**　　　) man.
   B We need to (**bu**　　　) up our funds from scratch.

📍 Phrase-Exercise

次の英文の（　）に適切な語句を語群から選びましょう（語形は必要に応じて変化させること）。

1. (   ) a crystal ball, the fortune-teller gave me some advice.

2. Pop stars are expected to be fashion-conscious and (   ) their appearances.

3. The painkillers were (   ) and the pain gradually got worse.

wear off　　look into　　addict to　　fall out of　　care about

📍 Composition-Exercise

[ ] の語句を使い、日本文の意味を表す英文を完成させましょう。

1. 医者は、治療中にその子供がよく我慢したので、彼にご褒美のアイスクリームをあげた。[reward, with]
   The doctor _____
   for being so patient when she treated him.

2. 「新しいビデオゲームはまったくすごいよ」─「道理で、彼がはまっているわけだ」
   [wonder, been addicted]
   "The new video game is simply terrific."─"_____
   _____ to it."

3. ゴマ油の臭いに我慢できないというのが、私が中華料理を食べない理由です。
   [why]
   I can't stand the smell of sesame oil, which _____
   _____.

Unit 6 Is Love an Addiction?

Summarizing-Exercise

以下は映像の要約です。（　　）に与えられた文字で始まる適語を入れて、文を完成させましょう。

　　We know how happy and hopeful we become when we fall in love with someone. But exactly what is happening in our mind on such an occasion? Surprisingly, the working of love is very similar to that of (**a**　　　) drugs, from the viewpoint of (**c**　　　) substance. Dopamine, for example, is (**r**　　　) when you experience or even expect pleasure of taking an addictive drug. It (**s**　　　) the reward system in the brain. The same is true with love: You are (**a**　　　) to a specific person and you want to see a lot of him/her. When you (**f**　　　) fall out of love, the (**c**　　　) becomes painful—the very serious blow that a lost love leads to. You can be relieved to know, however, oxytocin—one of the chemicals stimulating the (**r**　　　) system—now comes to the rescue in order to help recover such "addicts" out of their depression.

Stopover Dialogue

男女の短い会話を聞いて、以下の問題に答えましょう。

① 女性は男性の様子がおかしい原因を何だと考えていますか。

[　　　　　　　　　　　　　　　　　　　　　　　　　　　　]

② 男性の様子がおかしい本当の理由は何と推測されますか。

[　　　　　　　　　　　　　　　　　　　　　　　　　　　　]

③ あなたがこれまでで「中毒」と思えるほどに夢中になったものを3つ挙げてみましょう。

[　　　　　　　　　　　　　　　　　　　　　　　　　　　　]

Unit 7 Self-Driving Future
未来に向けたハイテク搭載車両

高齢ドライバーの免許自主返納が進まない背景には、自家用車が日常生活に不可欠という現実があります。そうした状況下で自動運転技術の早期実用化が返納を促進する可能性が指摘されています。最近の調査でも、自動運転車への高齢者の期待の高さが裏付けられています。多発する高齢ドライバーによる事故防止以外にも、未来に多くの可能性を含んだ自動運転車の開発は現在進行中です。

Word-Exercise

次の単語の意味を下のa～eから選びましょう。

Part I

1. overcome [ ]　2. harmless [ ]　3. pedestrian [ ]　4. futuristic [ ]
5. obstacle [ ]

a. 歩行者	b. 打ち勝つ	c. 無害の	d. 障害	e. 未来的な

Part II

1. vital [ ]　2. properly [ ]　3. depth [ ]　4. perspective [ ]
5. illuminate [ ]

a. 適切に	b. 照らす	c. 深さ	d. きわめて重要な	e. 視点

Pre-Study

以下は、車の各パーツを表したものです。1～10の空欄に適切な語句を記入しましょう。

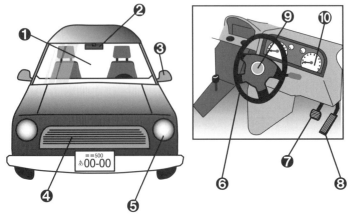

❶ w_____
❷ r_____ mirror
❸ s_____ mirror
❹ b_____
❺ h_____
❻ s_____ wheel
❼ b_____ pedal
❽ g_____ pedal
❾ h_____
❿ s_____

Unit 7　Self-Driving Future

1st Watch

映像の Part I、II を観て、1と2の英文が内容と一致していればTを、していなければFを○で囲みましょう。また、3と4の英文が正しい内容を表すように破線部に入る適切な語（句）を a～c から選びましょう。

Part I ▶

1. Self-driving cars don't require "eyes" that can recognize pedestrians. [T / F]
2. Carmakers still need to overcome obstacles before putting self-driving cars on the market. [T / F]
3. Self-driving cars are expected to work -------- a real person is driving.
    a. as if
    b. even if
    c. only if
4. The car must recognize obstacles ahead of us even --------.
    a. at a distance
    b. behind the wheel
    c. in sci-fi movies

Part II ▶▶

1. A LIDAR sensor would be essential equipment on a self-driving car. [T / F]
2. To cope with poor lighting or bad weather, the car also needs highly efficient 3-D cameras. [T / F]
3. Previously, it was a difficult problem to -------- at a time.
    a. identify pedestrians
    b. measure millions of pixels
    c. produce high-speed prototypes
4. The short strobe method allows researchers to measure the -------- in a flash.
    a. time and distance
    b. two million pixels
    c. whole area

43

▶ 2nd Watch

映像をもう一度観て、下線部に入る語句を記入して英文を完成させましょう。

Part I
DL 26　CD1-26

Reporter: The race to develop self-driving cars is on. We've already seen test-drive prototypes. And soon, some researchers argue, we could have robot cars acting as chauffeurs during our daily commutes, letting us sit back and read, text, email or watch TV while [1]_____.

But there are still challenges carmakers need to overcome before we see highways packed with autonomous vehicles; you know, the little things like mistaking harmless puddles of water for potholes. And then, there's the big stuff like misjudging the movements of a pedestrian and causing serious injury.

Now researchers are working to get self-driving cars to act as if [2]_____. To do that they need to be equipped with "eyes" and "brains" that work more like humans.

Reporter: To many people, the idea of self-driving cars is something of futuristic sci-fi movies. But [3]_____. And autonomous cars have the potential to transform the way we get around. But before we see rows of self-driving cars at the dealer, the technology behind the cars still has obstacles to overcome.

Paul Banks, President and Founder of TetraVue: The car needs to be able [4]_____, be able to recognize at a distance whether it's a piece of paper or whether it's a rock, whether it's a pothole. And the thing that makes it easiest for the car to be able to tell that is depth, distance.

Part II
DL 27　CD1-27

Reporter: To recognize depth and distance, most self-driving cars use similar technologies, with one vital piece of equipment being a LIDAR sensor. It maps objects in 3-D by bouncing laser beams off its surroundings, providing detailed maps the car needs to get around, and identifying objects like pedestrians and other vehicles.

But LIDAR isn't perfect in conditions like poor lighting at night or bad weather. This is why 3-D cameras that can process details from the world around them at high speeds and long distances, are key if the autonomous car industry is to properly take off.

35 **Banks:** [5]_____,
and being able to see something smaller than a car requires millions of pixels. From an optics perspective, it's great because we're able to use optics in a new way that allows us to measure what
40 has been a really difficult problem. And we've been successful in building prototypes and showing that we can really measure two million pixels at a time, out to 50 yards from the camera in snowstorms even, and [6] _____.

  We create the distance measurement by using a short strobe that illuminates
45 the whole area. The light comes back and then that's where we're able to [7] _____, and we do it all at once. So, it happens in a fraction of a microsecond. So our objective is within 12 to 24 months [to] have engineering samples or product prototypes [8] _____.

50 **Reporter:** This is Inside Science.

Notes
l.5 **chauffeurs**（自家用車のお抱え）運転手　l.11 **puddles of water** 水たまり　l.11 **potholes** 穴
l.11 **big stuff** 重要な物事、要素　l.26 **LIDAR** ライダー（Light Detection and Ranging〈光検出と測距〉の略称。LightとRadarを合わせた造語とも考えられている）

📍 Vocabulary Build-Up

次のA，Bの（　　）に、与えられた文字で始まる共通の単語を文中から探して記入し、文を完成させましょう（語形は必要に応じて変化させること）。

1. **A** I used to (**mi**　　　) Paul with his twin brother.
   B This dictionary contains a list of easily-(**mi**　　　) English words.

2. **A** They succeeded in (**tr**　　　) electricity into mechanical energy.
   B Bees collect nectar from the flowers and (**tr**　　　) it into honey.

3. **A** My counselor gave me some tips for (**ov**　　　) my depression.
   B The team (**ov**　　　) the psychological pressure and won first prize.

Phrase-Exercise

次の英文の（　）に適切な語句を語群から選びましょう（語形は必要に応じて変化させること）。

1. The business of AI is just starting to (　　　　　) in this small country.

2. World-famous temples in Kyoto are always heavily (　　　　　) tourists.

3. For a change, why don't we (　　　　　) by bus instead of subway today?

> pack with　　equip with　　get around　　take off　　come back

Composition-Exercise

[　]の語句を使い、日本文の意味を表す英文を完成させましょう。

1. もしこのビジネスで成功したいのなら、あなた方の協力が是非とも必要です。[to]
   Your cooperation is key if you are _____.

2. 彼の車にはドライブレコーダーとカーナビが装着されている。[dashboard camera]
   His car is _____ and a navigation system.

3. 医療業界におけるモバイル技術によって、私たちが手術を受ける方法が変わる可能性がある。[potential]
   Mobile technology in the medical industry _____
   _____ we undergo surgery.

Summarizing-Exercise

以下は映像の要約です。(　　) に与えられた文字で始まる適語を入れて、文を完成させましょう。

> Will autonomous vehicles appear on the market anytime soon? No, the time is not ripe yet. Car manufacturers have to (**o**　　) a couple of obstacles before robot cars take over driving for humans. In order to grasp its surroundings, the car needs to recognize "depth" and "distance" accurately. Today, most self-driving cars use a LIDAR (**s**　　) that allows the car to (**i**　　) and get around objects ahead such as pedestrians and other vehicles. However, LIDAR is not reliable enough in conditions like poor (**l**　　) or bad (**w**　　). So they have created high-performance 3-D cameras that can (**m**　　) millions of pixels even in snowstorms. Also, using short strobe technology, they can measure the distance in a (**f**　　) of a microsecond. Thanks to these devices, the dream of self-driving will come true before we know it.

Stopover Dialogue

ある男女が各自で考えた自動運転技術について話しています。この会話を聞いて、以下の問題に答えましょう。 ***note:*** **blood platelets**「血小板」

① 男性の考えた自動運転技術は、どんな場所で使われますか？

[　　]

② 女性の考えた自動運転技術は、どんな場所で使われますか？

[　　]

③ 身の回りで「自動運転」するものを３つ挙げてみましょう。次に、ペアを組んで「自動運転」が実現してほしいものを考えてみましょう。

[　　]

Unit 8 No Needle, No Thread?
自己修復する布の開発を目指して

生物には進化の過程で獲得した能力が備わっています。イカも例外ではありません。捕食に必要な「環歯」と呼ばれる吸盤内側の角質リングについているギザギザ部分がダメージを受けると、自己修復機能が働き始め、まもなく自らの力で「歯」を再生させることができるのです。吸盤で行われるこの再生の仕組みには、私たちの生活を便利にするヒントが隠されていることを科学者が発見しました。

Word-Exercise

次の単語の意味を下のa～eから選びましょう。

Part I
1. squid [ ] 2. tear [ ] 3. ragged [ ] 4. prey [ ] 5. flexible [ ]

   a. 獲物   b. 裂け目   c. ぼろぼろの   d. 柔軟性のある   e. イカ

Part II
1. fabric [ ] 2. mall [ ] 3. eliminate [ ] 4. synthetically [ ]
5. hazardous [ ]

   a. ショッピングセンター   b. 危険な   c. 排除する   d. 布（地）   e. 合成的に

Pre-Study

次の実験室のイラストにあるA～Gの器具の名称を英語で記入しましょう。

A:
B: test ( )
C: ( ) rack
D:
E: ( ) dish
F: glass ( )
G:

Unit 8 No Needle, No Thread?

▶ 1st Watch

映像の Part I、II を観て、1と2の英文が内容と一致していれば T を、していなければ F を○で囲みましょう。また、3と4の英文が正しい内容を表すように破線部に入る適切な語（句）を a ～ c から選びましょう。

Part I ▶

1. The squid has teeth inside of its suction cups.　　　　　　　　　　［T / F］
2. The teeth are made strong only with the aid of soft parts in the protein.
　　　　　　　　　　　　　　　　　　　　　　　　　　　　　　　　　［T / F］
3. The teeth ring structures help the squid --------.
    a. catch the prey
    b. keep tentacles and arms flexible
    c. mend a tear in a few seconds
4. As it turns out, the broken protein in the teeth of a squid will --------.
    a. stop it from taking a bite as soon as possible
    b. fuse back thanks to the soft parts in the protein
    c. try to reinforce the coating

Part II ▶▶

1. The unique properties of the protein enables you to repair any damage.
　　　　　　　　　　　　　　　　　　　　　　　　　　　　　　　　　［T / F］
2. We are still not quite likely to buy self-healing jeans at the mall.　　［T / F］
3. Researchers have already succeeded in growing the squid protein --------.
    a. in laboratories
    b. in the process of repair
    c. with a little pressure
4. Self-healing materials are more than helpful in --------.
    a. developing a coating in the heated water
    b. exposing people to real danger
    c. protecting people who work under hazardous conditions

▶ 2nd Watch

映像をもう一度観て、下線部に入る語句を記入して英文を完成させましょう。

Part I

Reporter: Got a ripped pair of jeans or T-shirt, but can't sew worth a dime? What if you could mend a tear in a few seconds with just water? [1] _____ _____ that might one day repair ragged clothes and other materials with a little pressure, heat, and H_2O.

Reporter: This [2] _____ for an order of calamari, but it's not. This species of squid have[has] teeth—yes, teeth. And scientists use them for research.

Abdon Pena-Francesch, PhD candidate (Pennsylvania State University): So in each of the tentacles and arms in, inside of, of the suction cups, there are, these are teeth ring structures that they use to catch the prey. They [3] _____ _____ they also, they also bite.

Reporter: It turns out that squid teeth contain a protein with soft and hard parts that work together to help make the teeth strong and flexible.

In the squid, if the teeth are broken, they can self-heal themselves. The soft parts in the proteins help the broken proteins fuse back together in water, while the hard parts help to reinforce the structure and [4] _____ _____. It's these unique properties that inspired scientists to develop a coating made from the squid teeth proteins.

Part II

Pena-Francesch: This protein, what is special about the, about this, this material, is that with a little bit of pressure, with a little bit of heat, [5] _____ _____.

Reporter: When a fabric covered in the coating is then soaked in water, the proteins move towards any rips or tears in the coating and link parts of the coating and fabric together to make repairs. Scientists also help the repair process along a little.

Pena-Francesch: ⁶_____, you put it back together with a little bit of, of heat and pressure, it's as good as new.

Reporter: But don't expect to see self-healing jeans and T-shirts at the mall just yet. Scientists need to work on large-scale production of the squid protein. They've already found ways to eliminate the need for using real squid.

Pena-Francesch: We can grow these proteins synthetically in the labs.

Reporter: These ground up lab-made proteins work ⁷_____ _____. Scientists also envision self-healing materials for hazardous materials suits where rips or tears could be a real danger, exposing people to hazardous things; a suit that repairs itself could help keep people safe. Science and nature coming together to ⁸_____. This is Inside Science.

Notes
l.2 **can't ~ worth a dime** 〜する値打ちはほとんどない　*l.10* **calamari**（食用に調理する）イカ
l.13 **tentacles** 触手　*l.13* **arms** 触腕（イカ類が持つ、獲物を捕らえるのに使う他の触手よりも長い2本の触手）
l.13 **suction cups** 吸盤　*l.19* **fuse back together** 溶け合って元通りに一体になる　*l.30* **rips** 裂け目
l.40 **envision** 構想する

◉ Vocabulary Build-Up

次のA，Bの（　）に、与えられた文字で始まる共通の単語を文中から探して記入し、文を完成させましょう（語形は必要に応じて変化させること）。

1. **A** Hackers have (**ex**　　　) the personal data of the company's 110-million customers.
   B Smokers are (**ex**　　　) people every single day to secondhand smoke.

2. **A** Caught in a rain shower, my clothes were (**so**　　　) wet and I was chilled to the bone.
   B The nurse picked up an alcohol-(**so**　　　) gauze just before giving me a shot.

3. **A** Some (**re**　　　) are needed to play my guitar in the basement.
   B I tried (**re**　　　) my printer by myself but it went from bad to worse.

Phrase-Exercise

次の英文の（　）に適切な語句を語群から選びましょう（語形は必要に応じて変化させること）。

1. (　　　　　　　　) a teenager, I'm always asked to show ID in a liquor shop.

2. Many issues (　　　　　　　　) last week prolonged the meeting.

3. My skin is so sensitive that most of my clothes are (　　　　　　　　) 100% natural materials.

| work on | look like | make from | move towards | come together |

Composition-Exercise

[　]の語句を使い、日本文の意味を表す英文を完成させましょう。

1. セロリには食物繊維がたくさん含まれていることがわかった。[turned]
   _____ celery contains a lot of dietary fiber.

2. まさにこの抗体の特性が科学者たちに新薬の開発を思いつかせた。[inspired]
   It is this property of the antibody that _____
   _____ .

3. この細胞の特別なところは、実験室で育成できる点だ。[what]
   _____ is that it can be grown in a lab.

Summarizing-Exercise

DL 32 CD2-04

以下は映像の要約です。（　　　）に与えられた文字で始まる適語を入れて、文を完成させましょう。

Researchers are working on a dream coating material that could patch up tears in your clothes in a few seconds. They were (i   ) to develop such material by observing a species of squid. The squid has teeth inside of its suction cups. Yes, they will bite as well as suction their (p   ). And if the teeth are broken, a unique protein enables them to heal themselves. The soft part of the protein (f   ) back together the broken teeth and the hard part of it keeps them strong. Together they complete the repair. It is from this squid teeth protein that the researchers developed a cloth-repair coating. First, cover the (f   ) with the coating and secondly (s   ) it in water, and the protein will start making repairs on its own. The protein can be produced on a large scale in the lab, so you need not catch lots of real squid. Also scientists envision self-(h   ) suits for people who are exposed to (h   ) things.

Stopover Dialogue

DL 33 CD2-05

男女がジーンズのある問題について話しています。この会話を聞いて、以下の問題に答えましょう。

① ジーンズの問題とは何ですか。〔　　　　　　　　　　　　　　　　　　　〕
② ①の問題に対処するために女性はどのような技術を提案しましたか。
〔　　　　　　　　　　　　　　　　　　　　　　　　　　　　　　　　　　〕
③ ほかに、生物の特性を技術や商品開発に応用した例を調べましょう。

生　物	特　性	具体的な応用例

Unit 9 Aiming for a Perfect Squeeze
ハスに学ぶムダのない生活

ハスの葉の撥水性、いわゆる「ロータス効果」を研究するアメリカの科学者チームは、水だけを通して油をはじくナノテク素材を2015年に開発しました。原油流出事故の対応や地中での石油探査に役立つものとして現在、実用化一歩手前です。この発表に続いて同チームは、ロータス効果を応用した最新の研究成果を公表しました。今回は、私たちの日常生活に密接にかかわる研究です。

◉ Word-Exercise

次の単語の意味を下のa〜eから選びましょう。

Part I ▶

1. squeeze [　]　2. annoying [　]　3. detergent [　]　4. dirt [　]　5. droplet [　]

| a. 泥 | b. いらだたしい | c. 搾る | d. 洗剤 | e. 小滴 |

Part II ▶▶

1. laundry [　]　2. uncoated [　]　3. slide [　]　4. once [　]　5. store [　]

| a. 未加工の | b. 滑る | c. 保管する | d. いったん〜すると | e. 洗濯 |

◉ Pre-Study

次は物質の状態変化を表したものです。A〜Fに当てはまる語句を語群から選びましょう。

- freezing
- gas
- melting
- evaporation
- sublimation
- solid

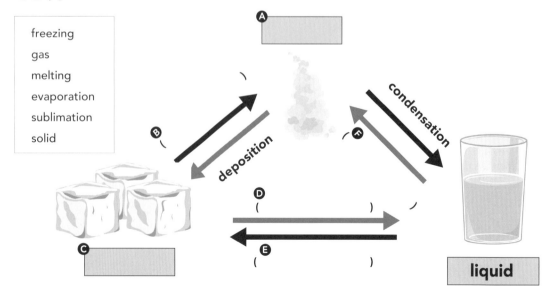

54

Unit 9 Aiming for a Perfect Squeeze

▶ 1st Watch

映像の Part I、II を観て、1と2の英文が内容と一致していればTを、していなければFを○で囲みましょう。また、3と4の英文が正しい内容を表すように破線部に入る適切な語（句）をa～cから選びましょう。

Part I ▶

1. We are sometimes frustrated at the results of scientific researches. [T / F]
2. When you can't squeeze every drop of shampoo from the bottle, you feel like you've wasted your money. [T / F]
3. Shampoo is good at -------- dirt with aid of the chemicals called surfactants.
   a. clinging to
   b. getting around
   c. sticking by
4. -------- the lotus leaf, scientists have invented a new type of coating.
   a. Made of
   b. Left behind
   c. Inspired by

Part II ▶▶

1. No shampoo or detergent can hold onto an uncoated surface. [T / F]
2. The lotus-like coating is guaranteed to repel liquid for a very long time. [T / F]
3. Before the bottles with new coating appear on the market, it would be a good idea to keep --------.
   a. repelling the liquid quickly
   b. sliding shampoo off the surface
   c. storing bottles upside down
4. It is the psychology of consumerism to expect to use the contents of the bottle to the --------.
   a. good shake
   b. last drop
   c. uncoated surfaces

55

▶ 2nd Watch

映像をもう一度観て、下線部に入る語句を記入して英文を完成させましょう。

Part I　　　　　　　　　　　　　　　　　　　DL 34　　CD2-06

Reporter: Sometimes science solves longstanding mysteries like gravitational waves, or finds one of the fundamental building blocks of the universe called top quarks.

　Or sometimes science just helps with some of life's little frustrations, like getting the last drop of shampoo out of the bottle. Scientists have invented 1_____, so getting every last drop out is finally achievable.

Reporter: There's just no getting around it. No matter how much you squeeze or shake a shampoo bottle, there's always going to be some left behind.

Bharat Bhushan PhD (Ohio State University): It's annoying to consumer. And you look at your cap, cap is filthy. It collects the shampoo or the detergent, and also you're not able to 2_____ out of the bottle, which means you're throwing money away.

Reporter: But how does shampoo stick to the bottle anyway? The chemicals that make shampoo good at clinging to the dirt in your hair, called surfactants, also make it good at sticking to surfaces like the inside of a bottle.

Bhushan: To develop a coating which will repel shampoo, repellent, and a variety of oils, we're 3_____.

Reporter: The lotus leaf's bumpy surface, which lets liquids roll right off, led the researchers at the Ohio State University to create a coating for the inside of bottles made of tiny nanoparticles. If you could look at the coating under a microscope, you would see tiny "Y"s that cradle droplets of shampoo, which are balanced on top of 4_____. This minimizes the contact between the shampoo and the inside of the shampoo bottle.

Part II　　　　　　　　　　　　　　　　　　　DL 35　　CD2-07

Reporter: Watch as shampoo and laundry detergent 5_____
_____. Now watch as shampoo and detergent slide right off a surface treated with the new coating.

Bhushan: We can create a structure which will repel liquid but we'd like to make

sure it does it ⁶_____
_____.

Reporter: Once the coating is perfected, it will be several years before we can buy products that use the coating in their bottles. So, until then, keep storing bottles upside down or ⁷_____
_____.

Bhushan: So I think it's important from the consumer point of view. The consumer would like to get the last drop of the liquid out, which ⁸_____
_____.

Reporter: Science to help you get every last drop for every last buck. This is Inside Science.

Notes
l.2 **gravitational waves** 重力波　l.5 **quarks** クォーク（物質の基本的構成要素。素粒子グループのひとつ）
l.14 **filthy** 汚れている　l.18 **surfactants** 界面活性剤　l.20 **repel** はじく　l.20 **repellent** 防水剤
l.24 **nanoparticle** ナノ粒子　l.43 **buck** ドル（dollarの俗語）

Vocabulary Build-Up

次のA, Bの（　）に、与えられた文字で始まる共通の単語を文中から探して記入し、文を完成させましょう（語形は必要に応じて変化させること）。

1. **A** When the girl offered her hand to him, he hesitated to (**sh**　　　) hands.
   B My mother finally (**sh**　　　) off her prejudice against comics and allowed me to buy some.

2. **A** (**Th**　　　) away by his sweetheart, he decided to leave his hometown.
   B Children are enjoying (**th**　　　) snowballs into their friends' faces.

3. **A** (**St**　　　) in heavy traffic, we missed the opening ceremony.
   B A spoonful of olive oil prevents the noodles from (**st**　　　).

Phrase-Exercise

次の英文の（　）に適切な語句を語群から選びましょう（語形は必要に応じて変化させること）。

1. Fortunately the rescue team have found a man (　　　　　) the rock.

2. I'm planning to (　　　　　) volunteer work in disaster-affected areas this summer.

3. Her academic scores were so excellent that her tuition has been (　　　　　) by the university

help with　　leave behind　　cling to　　treat with　　pay for

Composition-Exercise

[　] の語句を使い、日本文の意味を表す英文を完成させましょう。

1. 消費税を合法的に逃れるすべはありません。[getting]
   There is ＿＿＿＿＿＿＿＿＿＿＿＿＿＿＿ the consumption tax legally.

2. ロータス・コーティング処理をされたボードの表面を雪が滑り落ちるのをごらんください。[slide]
   Watch the snow ＿＿＿＿＿＿＿＿＿＿＿＿＿
   that is treated with lotus-coating.

3. 空気圧を高めれば、タイヤと路面の接触は最小限になります。[contact]
   Make the air pressure high, and the ＿＿＿＿＿＿＿＿＿＿
   ＿＿＿＿＿＿＿＿＿＿ is minimized.

Summarizing-Exercise

以下は映像の要約です。（　　　）に与えられた文字で始まる適語を入れて、文を完成させましょう。

> You try to squeeze the last drop of the shampoo or detergent out of a bottle, but you are always annoyed to find some liquid left (**s**　　　) to the inner surface of the container.
>
> As a solution to this problem, the scientists focus on the self-cleaning effect of the lotus leaf. Getting a hint from this, they succeeded in developing a new (**c**　　　) to be applied to the inside of bottles, which various types of liquid will (**r**　　　) off. The key parts of this nanoparticle coating are Y-shaped cradles and tiny air (**b**　　　) which work together to sustain droplets of the liquid and prevent them from (**c**　　　) to the surface. Within a few years, you will be able to (**s**　　　) the last drop and money out of the bottle!

Stopover Dialogue

女性が着用しているマスクについて男女が話しています。この会話を聞いて、以下の問題に答えましょう。

notes: **odor**「匂い（主に悪臭）」　**dissolve**「分解する」　**bead up**「球状になる」

① 女性は何のためにマスクを着けていますか。

[　　　　　　　　　　　　　　　　　　　　　　　　]

② 女性のマスクは具体的にどんな働きをしますか。

[　　　　　　　　　　　　　　　　　　　　　　　　]

③ 「ロータス効果」が応用できそうな他の例を考えてみましょう。

[　　　　　　　　　　　　　　　　　　　　　　　　]

Unit 10 Identifying Fake Drugs
偽造薬を見破るアプリ

近年、深刻な社会問題を引き起こしている偽造薬は、驚くほど精巧に造られています。外見を基準にせざるを得ない人間の目に代わって判別に威力を発揮するのは、中身を直視できる科学の目です。偽造薬の被害が急増しているアメリカでは、分光法を利用し、薬の原形を損なうことなく成分を可視化するアプリケーションの開発が進んでいます。偽造薬根絶への大きな一歩です。

Word-Exercise

次の単語の意味を下のa～eから選びましょう。

Part I

1. regulation [ ]　2. enforcement [ ]　3. shortage [ ]　4. profit [ ]
5. spot [ ]

| a. 利益を得る | b. 不足 | c. 施行 | d. 規制 | e. 見抜く |

Part II

1. analyze [ ]　2. ongoing [ ]　3. genuine [ ]　4. confirm [ ]　5. ultimate [ ]

| a. 継続的な | b. 本物の | c. 究極の | d. 確認する | e. 解析する |

Pre-Study

薬にはいろいろな形態があります。例を参考に、1～5の写真に相当する語を与えられた文字をヒントに記入してみましょう。

例 (cream / ointment)

(**ta**　　　　　　)

(**ca**　　　　　　)

(**po**　　　　　　)

(**sy**　　　　　　)

(**dr**　　　　　　)

Unit 10 Identifying Fake Drugs

▶ 1st Watch

映像の Part I、II を観て、1と2の英文が内容と一致していれば T を、していなければ F を○で囲みましょう。また、3と4の英文が正しい内容を表すように破線部に入る適切な語（句）を a～c から選びましょう。

Part I ▶

1. In developing countries, the regulation of fake drugs is not strict enough. [T / F]
2. Some consumers will profit from buying fake pharmaceuticals. [T / F]
3. Most consumers could not -------- genuine drugs from fake one at first glance.
   a. exceed
   b. look
   c. tell
4. Counterfeiters have made a huge profit, while many people who chose to take counterfeit medicines --------.
   a. could have easy access to medical care
   b. have died from their harmful effects
   c. suffer from shortage of drugs

Part II ▶▶

1. It is impossible to analyze a drug chemically before patients take it. [T / F]
2. Scientists have tried unsuccessfully to develop an application for a nondestructive test of drugs. [T / F]
3. Until recently, you had to -------- a pill first to test it.
   a. apply for
   b. crush up
   c. talk to
4. The spectrometer has analysis routines --------.
   a. built in it
   b. confirmed genuine
   c. expanded worldwide

▶ 2nd Watch

映像をもう一度観て、下線部に入る語句を記入して英文を完成させましょう。

Part I

Reporter: The World Health Organization reports that counterfeit medicines could make up [1]_____ _____ sold on the global market, with a large amount of fake drugs being bought and sold in developing countries.

Whether due to loose regulation or lax law enforcement, counterfeiters can run wild in poor countries. [2]_____ and many people seek inexpensive treatment options. Others are simply trying to survive with limited access to care. Many die making that choice. The only people who profit from fake pharmaceuticals are the counterfeiters.

Matt Keller (a research scientist at Intellectual Ventures Laboratory): The market of these counterfeit or substandard drugs could, could very well exceed a billion dollars every year.

Reporter: Now, a simple technology may be able to spot the fakes.

Reporter: [3]_____, can you tell the difference between these two drugs? Neither can most consumers.

Keller: If you just hold fake and genuine packets of drugs next to each other, just looking at them, the counterfeiters have gotten quite good at, you know, just [4]_____.

Part II

Reporter: Researchers like Keller are looking for ways to analyze drugs before they [5]_____ _____.

Keller: So, you might have to, for example, kind of crush up the pill, mix it with a chemical and kind of put it on a paper readout strip. But, the thing we like about spectroscopy is it's nondestructive. [6]_____. So, you buy your device and use a phone app that's basically all that you need. We developed an app that basically just talks to the spectrometer. It has prebuilt in analysis routines and then, it tells you, first of all, ⁷_____? And if it's genuine, then it confirms what the ingredient is.

Reporter: Researchers are working to expand the use of the app and test it in Southeast Asia, in areas where counterfeit drugs are a huge problem.

Keller: The ultimate goal is to basically have people taking drugs ⁸_____.

Reporter: This is Inside Science.

Notes
l.8 **lax** ゆるい　*l.9* **run wild** 野放しになる　*l.12* **pharmaceuticals** 薬剤　*l.14* **substandard drugs** 品質不良医薬品　*l.27* **kind of** 何と言うか、まぁ言ってみれば　*l.28* **paper readout strip** データ読み出しのための短冊状紙片　*l.29* **spectroscopy** 分光法（後出の spectrometer は「分光計」）　*l.29* **nondestructive** 非破壊の　*l.32* **talk to ~** ~にデータを送信する　*l.32* **analysis routines** 解析用ルーチン（ルーチンとはIT用語で、プログラム中のひとまとまりの機能を持つ命令群のこと）

♀Vocabulary Build-Up

次のA, Bの（　）に、与えられた文字で始まる共通の単語を文中から探して記入し、文を完成させましょう（語形は必要に応じて変化させること）。

1. **A** Some Chinese medicines are supposed to reduce the risk of (**de**   ) hay fever.
   B Nowadays many industrial robots are (**de**   ) in university laboratories.

2. **A** I'm sorry to say but I can't make a discount (**ex**   ) 10%.
   B Last year her expenses (**ex**   ) her income by far.

3. **A** Our new manager was determined to (**ex**   ) our customer base through better marketing.
   B We have to be careful about the rapidly (**ex**   ) sharing of information by SNS.

Phrase-Exercise

次の英文の（　）に適切な語句を語群から選びましょう（語形は必要に応じて変化させること）。

1. In spite of the bad weather, the runner continued the race and (　　　　　　　) the goal.

2. The Nagoya branch of our company (　　　　　　　) 30% of all sales last year.

3. The money brokers planned to (　　　　　　　) illegal financial transactions.

| make up | profit from | look for | crush up | make it to |

Composition-Exercise

[　]の語句を使い、日本文の意味を表す英文を完成させましょう。

1. あなたはバターとマーガリンの違いがわかりますか。[tell]
   _____ butter and margarine?

2. より多くの人々が健康的な食を選択肢として求めるので、ベジタリアンレストランの需要が不足することはありません。[demand]
   There is _____
   as more people seek healthy eating options.

3. 医療へのアクセスが限られている人々にとって、この薬はよりよい選択肢となるでしょう。[limited]
   This drug will be a better option for people who have _____
   _____.

Summarizing-Exercise

以下は映像の要約です。(　　　) に与えられた文字で始まる適語を入れて、文を完成させましょう。

> According to the WHO, more than 50 percent of the medicines sold worldwide are not authentic. A large amount of these fake medicines are sold in (**d**　　　) countries. Many people in these countries are poor, and in addition, their access to (**m**　　　) care is limited. Consequently, they have little choice but to buy (**c**　　　) drugs, which are inexpensive but can be fatal.
>
> How can we tell genuine drugs from fake ones that look so real at first (**g**　　　)? Traditionally, you had to (**c**　　　) up the pill and test it by causing a chemical reaction with other substances. However, a newly developed spectroscopy (**a**　　　) would give you quicker results. The device has a built-in (**a**　　　) program. You have only to put on the drug on the device and it will instantly let you know whether the drug is genuine or not.

Stopover Dialogue

男女がスイカ (watermelon) の選び方について話しています。この会話を聞いて、以下の問題に答えましょう。

notes: **electromagnetic**「電磁気の」　**ultrasonic**「超音波の」

① 女性の持っているアプリはどんな働きをしますか。

[　　　　　　　　　　　　　　　　　　　　　　　　　　]

② NDT とは何の略ですか。

[　　　　　　　　　　　　　　　　　　　　　　　　　　]

③ NDT が実際に使われている例にどんなものがあるかを調べてみましょう。

[　　　　　　　　　　　　　　　　　　　　　　　　　　]

Unit 11 Sensory Judgement is Important

ヒット商品の鍵を握るサイコレオロジー

科学の進歩は時に新しい学問分野を生み出しますが、サイコレオロジーはその一例です。「サイコロジー」と「レオロジー」の合成語という成り立ちが示すとおり、サイコレオロジーは、変形と流動に関わる科学的性質に対する心の動きを研究する学問で、化粧品や食品業界を中心に、商品開発に役立つ研究として注目されています。心をくすぐる商品が、今後増えてくるかもしれません。

Word-Exercise

次の単語の意味を下のa～eから選びましょう。

Part I

1. likewise [　]　2. texture [　]　3. perception [　]　4. aesthetics [　]
5. noticeable [　]

a. 気づき得る　b. 手ざわり　c. 同様に　d. 知覚　e. 美観

Part II

1. evaluate [　]　2. questionnaire [　]　3. preference [　]　4. pupil [　]
5. sensory [　]

a. 好み　b. 評価する　c. アンケート　d. 感覚の　e. 瞳

Pre-Study

食感にはいろいろな表現があります。写真と説明をヒントに、1～5の食感を表す語を語群から選びましょう。

Texture of Food

1. _____

2. _____

3. _____

4. _____

5. _____

food that makes a grinding noise when bitten

food that is quite hard to chew

food that is a little wet

food that is easy to chew

food that has been fried in oil

moist　tender　tough　greasy　crunchy

Unit 11 Sensory Judgement is Important

▶ 1st Watch

映像の Part I、II を観て、1と2の英文が内容と一致していればTを、していなければFを○で囲みましょう。また、3と4の英文が正しい内容を表すように破線部に入る適切な語（句）をa～cから選びましょう。

Part I ▶

1. The reporter heard of psychorheology many times before. [T / F]
2. Psychorheology deals with how a product feels when you touch it. [T / F]
3. Companies know that consumers are -------- the texture of their product.
    a. responsible for
    b. paying attention to
    c. in favor of
4. With regard to products, it is so hard to bridge the -------- gap between scientists and consumers.
    a. measurement
    b. aesthetic
    c. noticeable

Part II ▶▶

1. The consumer experience is essential when launching a new product. [T / F]
2. A good fragrance is an important quality in a new lotion. [T / F]
3. The consumers' response can be evaluated by --------, for example.
    a. eye tracking
    b. measuring product sizes
    c. the sense of taste
4. Companies are very much alert to --------.
    a. how they can profit from their products
    b. what the consumers really prefer
    c. whether the consumers are measuring their reactions

▶ 2nd Watch

映像をもう一度観て、下線部に入る語句を記入して英文を完成させましょう。

Part I 　　　　　　　　　　　　　　　DL 42　CD2-14

Reporter: I love learning about a new field of science. It's like finding a new book by a great author or discovering that your favorite restaurant has a special tasting room upstairs—like it's been there all the time but [1]_____.

The field of psychorheology is like that for me. Most of my life, I had never heard of it. But [2]_____ I reap its benefits in many everyday consumer products, everything from hot cocoa to sunscreen.

Psychorheology touches upon how products feel—or more specifically, how we feel when we touch products. That makeup, that hand lotion—is it oily, dry, smooth, stiff, rough, thick, light or foamy?

Companies care about these things because consumers care. We [3]_____ _____, a certain color, a certain scent. And likewise, we seek a certain texture. How does it feel? That's exactly what psychorheology seeks to achieve.

Matjaz Jogan, PhD (Johnson & Johnson): This work is about a perception, human perception of this quality. The question is how do our consumers perceive a product in terms of how thick they are.

Jeffrey Martin (Johnson & Johnson): Our projects started when I would get many, many scientists who were making formulations and they would come to me and say, "I'm trying to match the aesthetics of a product that is [4]_____ _____, and I have a few different prototypes and so I would run many different measurements." Of course, it's never going to match exactly, so I would have to go back to them and say, "Well, here's a prototype that matches very close." And then I would always get that question, "Is the difference noticeable by the consumer?" and I would always have to answer, "I don't know."

Part II 　　　　　　　　　　　　　　　DL 43　CD2-15

Jogan: We want the consumer to be happy with the product. So, the consumer experience is very important. And we can [5]_____

68

_____ by basically measuring it by questionnaires or also by measuring their preferences. For measuring their preferences, we can use different tools like eye tracking, you know, measuring their pupil sizes, and so on, on ⁶_____.

Martin: All of the different sensory cues for a certain product type are very important. You can have a lotion that we can show through data that really delivers of very good benefit, and it can have very good aesthetics, but if it doesn't have a good fragrance it's not going ⁷_____.

Jogan: Like having more and more data and merchant models, we should be closer to what the consumer in the end really wants. Especially now that the consumer preferences are changing ⁸_____.

Notes
l.8 **psychorheology** サイコレオロジー（物質の流動や変形の研究を行うレオロジーの応用分野で、手ざわりやのどごしなど化粧品や食品分野の感性を扱う）　*l.9* **reap its benefits** その恩恵を受ける　*l.15* **scent** 芳香　*l.22* **making formulations** 試作品を作る　*l.25* **run many different measurements** さまざまな計測を実施する

◉Vocabulary Build-Up

次のA, Bの（　）に、与えられた文字で始まる共通の単語を文中から探して記入し、文を完成させましょう（語形は必要に応じて変化させること）。

1. **A** Some behaviors are (**pe**　　　) differently according to gender.
   B Being so optimistic, she tends to (**pe**　　　) everything as good luck.

2. **A** No one can (**ma**　　　) him in playing tennis.
   B The doctors spent much time in (**ma**　　　) donors and recipients.

3. **A** Their English abilities are (**me**　　　) by multiple-choice tests.
   B Dr. Parker is now engaged in (**me**　　　) the brain activity of the rat.

Phrase-Exercise

次の英文の（　）に適切な語句を語群から選びましょう（語形は必要に応じて変化させること）。

1. Have you ever (　　　　　　　) the superstition—"it's bad luck when a black cat crosses your path"?

2. (　　　　　　　) at the night sky, the children tried to find the Milky Way.

3. The failure of the experiment forced us to (　　　　　　　) the first stage of the research.

| look up   come to   touch on   hear of   go back to |

Composition-Exercise

[　]の語句を使い、日本文の意味を表す英文を完成させましょう。

1. 彼女は論文の中で、消費者の好みをどう評価したかについて触れました。
   [touched / how]

   _____

   consumers' preferences in her article.

2. 絹のなめらかな手触りこそがまさに私たちの手に入れたいものなのです。
   [texture]

   _____

   is exactly what we seek to achieve.

3. 彼らは、新製品についてのアンケート結果に満足しました。[happy]

   _____

   about the new product.

Unit 11 Sensory Judgement is Important

Summarizing-Exercise   DL 44   CD2-16

以下は映像の要約です。（　　　）に与えられた文字で始まる適語を入れて、文を完成させましょう。

Companies that launch a new product have always (**c**　　　) about whether the consumer will like its appearance, color, or flavor, etc. and whether or not the consumer will be satisfied. Now the companies are also taking into consideration another aspect of (**s**　　　) cues: how consumers feel about the texture of the product. Does it have a stiff touch or feel like foam? Is it (**o**　　　), sticky, or dry? This is a rather new field of science called psychorheology.

All these (**a**　　　) qualities may vary from one (**f**　　　) to another, but companies try to consider them so that a new product will suit the consumer's liking. And the (**m**　　　) of a product's texture is one key feature now. This is a growing trend.

Stopover Dialogue   DL 45   CD2-17

男女がシュークリーム（cream puff）について話しています。この会話を聞いて、以下の問題に答えましょう。 ***notes:*** **floury**「ぱさついている」 **impaired**「十分に機能していない」

① 女性は、おもにシュークリームのどこに注目していますか。

② なぜ男性はシュークリームの「舌触り」を気にしているのですか。

③ ペアを組んで、身の回りにある「見た目」「味」「舌触り」など、五感のいろいろな働きに訴えかける商品の例をいくつか挙げてみましょう。

Unit 12 Dangerous Debris in Space
ゴミのない安全な宇宙空間を

ゴミ問題が深刻なのは、地上に限ったことではありません。人工衛星などへの衝突事故を招く宇宙ゴミも除去を急がなければなりません。宇宙開発の負の遺産とも言える宇宙ゴミの回収に関して、各国の科学者が知恵を絞り、次々と実験が行われているのが現在の状況です。科学者を味方につけた宇宙のクリーンアップ活動はこの瞬間にも行われています。

◉ Word-Exercise

次の単語の意味を下の a ～ e から選びましょう。

Part I

1. junk [ ]　2. abandoned [ ]　3. marble [ ]　4. fleck [ ]　5. replace [ ]

a. ビー玉　b. 取り換える　c. がらくた　d. 小片　e. 見捨てられた

Part II

1. inevitable [ ]　2. mass [ ]　3. withstand [ ]　4. diameter [ ]
5. potential [ ]

a. 質量　b. 耐える　c. 見込み　d. 直径　e. 避けられない

◉ Pre-Study

宇宙に関連する次の①～④の写真に相当する語句を指定された文字と語数で書いてみましょう。

_ p _ _ _ _ _ _ t

s _ _ e _ _ _ _ _

_ e _ _ r

_ s _ r _ n _ _ _

Unit 12 Dangerous Debris in Space

▶ 1st Watch

映像の Part I、II を観て、1 と 2 の英文が内容と一致していれば T を、していなければ F を○で囲みましょう。また、3 と 4 の英文が正しい内容を表すように破線部に入る適切な語（句）を a ～ c から選びましょう。

Part I ▶

1. Looking up at the night sky, you can see lots of trash orbiting Earth.
   [T / F]
2. Many millions of pieces of space junk are too small to be tracked easily.
   [T / F]
3. Nobody will pay attention to the pieces of space junk, as they are now --------.
   a. floating around   **b.** hard to track   **c.** non-functioning
4. The pieces of debris travel at such high speeds that even a small object could --------.
   a. be abandoned sooner or later
   b. destroy a working spacecraft
   c. not be a mounting problem

Part II ▶▶

1. Today, so many pieces of debris are orbiting Earth that a collision between them is unlikely.   [T / F]
2. Laser polarimetry can help determine which country made the space junk.
   [T / F]
3. Researchers at MIT are making contributions to the --------.
   a. growing number of debris
   b. damage-causing collision
   c. space trash tracking mission
4. The International Space Station is -------- debris impact up to about one centimeter in diameter.
   a. able to avoid
   b. keeping an eye on
   c. tightly guarded against

▶ 2nd Watch

映像をもう一度観て、下線部に入る語句を記入して英文を完成させましょう。

Part I　　　　　　　　　🎧 DL 46　💿 CD2-18

Reporter: When you look up at the sky on a clear night, you might be able to see stars and a planet if you're lucky. But what you don't see is all the space junk that's up there [1]_____. Most of it is useless bits and pieces of stuff like [2]_____, abandoned launch crafts and old satellites that no one cares about anymore.

This space trash is traveling at over 17,000 miles per hour, plenty [3]_____ to working satellites and the International Space Station. NASA and the Department of Defense are keeping an eye on the debris, but now MIT researchers are helping the tracking efforts with a pretty cool laser.

Reporter: There are more than 20,000 pieces of space junk larger than a softball orbiting the Earth. There are over 500,000 pieces of debris the size of a marble or larger. And there are many millions of pieces of space trash that are so small they can't be tracked.

Even tiny flecks of paint can damage a spacecraft when traveling at such high speeds. In the past, [4]_____ have been replaced because of damage caused by paint flecks. Michael Pasqual at MIT has been watching this mounting problem.

Part II　　　　　　　　　🎧 DL 47　💿 CD2-19

Michael Pasqual PhD (Massachusetts Institute of Technology): So, initially it wasn't that big of a problem, but it is grown over time and now it is actually so crowded in space with debris that collisions with debris, between operational satellites and other debris, is sort of inevitable. The collision problem is [5]_____ in space. Even a piece of debris as small as a baseball could completely torpedo a satellite and

destroy it.

Reporter: The U.S. already uses telescopes and laser radars to keep an eye on the growing number and ⁶_____.

Now, engineers at MIT are using a technique called laser polarimetry to help with the space trash tracking mission. It can identify what the junk is made of, and help determine its mass and ⁷_____. The information could help NASA predict damage-causing impacts and move satellites out of the way.

Right now, the International Space Station is the most heavily protected spacecraft. It can withstand impacts from debris about one centimeter in diameter. If the pilots know a larger object is headed their way, ⁸_____. Laser technologies can help identify that bigger, damaging space junk.

Pasqual: We care a lot about difficult space problems, and space debris is one of the most critical problems that the country and the world will face in the near future. And applying very exciting technologies with lasers, it has a lot of potential there to tackle this difficult problem.

Reporter: This is Inside Science.

Notes
l.7 **bits and pieces** こまごまとしたもの *l.8* **launch crafts** 打ち上げ用ロケット *l.12* **Department of Defense** アメリカ国防総省 *l.27* **collisions with ~** ～との衝突 *l.31* **torpedo** 破壊する *l.35* **polarimetry** 偏光解析

◉Vocabulary Build-Up

次のA, Bの（　）に、与えられた文字で始まる共通の単語を文中から探して記入し、文を完成させましょう（語形は必要に応じて変化させること）。

1. **A** As I (**gr**   ) older, I became forgetful.
   B We have to work harder to meet the fast-(**gr**   ) demand of our customers.

2. **A** I kept silent, (**av**   ) a quarrel with him.
   B Some infectious diseases can be (**av**   ) by vaccination.

3. **A** The expedition team (**he**   ) in the wrong direction and got lost.
   B We have been waiting for the train (**he**   ) for London for one hour.

Phrase-Exercise

次の英文の（　）に適切な語句を語群から選びましょう（語形は必要に応じて変化させること）。

1. Our laboratory consists of ten members (　　　　　) a variety of fields.

2. Investors have (　　　　　) the new technology that could transform the solar power industry.

3. A rumor about her promotion is already (　　　　　) the office.

float around　care about　collide with　keep an eye on　come from

Composition-Exercise

[　] の語句を使い、日本文の意味を表す英文を完成させましょう。

1. その建物に閉じ込められた人々を救助するために、彼らは廃棄された車をどかさなければなりませんでした。[abandoned / way]
   To rescue people trapped in the building, they had to _____
   _____.

2. 一片の塗料でさえ、高速で進むときは、一個の衛星を破壊することが可能でしょう。[traveling]
   Even a fleck of paint could destroy a satellite _____
   _____.

3. この情報は、研究者が機能を終えた衛星を追跡するのに役立つでしょう。[track]
   The information could help _____.

Unit 12　Dangerous Debris in Space

Summarizing-Exercise　　DL 48　CD2-20

以下は映像の要約です。(　　　) に与えられた文字で始まる適語を入れて、文を完成させましょう。

　　Today, a lot of space junk is (**o**　　　　) Earth and varies in size. There are more than 500,000 objects that are smaller than a softball but larger than a (**m**　　　　), and there are many more that are too small to identify. These objects, including (**a**　　　　) space rockets and satellites, are travelling so fast that accidental (**c**　　　　) between them may happen at any time. Now researchers are trying to (**p**　　　　) such damage-causing (**i**　　　　) with the aid of laser technology. Laser polarimetry, for example, can identify the composition of the junk as well as help determine its (**m**　　　　) and where it came from. Lasers can be used to deal with these difficult space problems.

Stopover Dialogue　　DL 49　CD2-21

男女が天文台 (astronomical observatory) について話しています。この会話を聞いて、以下の問題に答えましょう。

notes: eruption「噴火」　villains「敵、悪者」

① 女性が言う天文台に対する４つ脅威のうち、述べられていないのはどれですか。
〔　宇宙ゴミ　　テロや窃盗などの人災　　自然災害　　人工的な光による干渉　　電磁波　〕

② 男性によれば、①の脅威を回避する方法とはどんなものですか。

［　　　］

③ 天文台には世界時刻の基準になったものがあります。ペアを組み、それがどこの、何という天文台かを調べて、その他わかったことを書いてみましょう。

［　　　］

Unit 13 A Safer Mission to Mars

火星の過酷なミッションを助ける新素材とは？

手のひらに乗せておくとドロドロと溶けだす水溶き片栗粉が、握ると一気に固くなる—こうした実験をテレビで見たことはありませんか。ダイラタンシーと呼ばれる現象を体験する実験ですが、こうした物質の性質を応用し、ナノテクノロジーと組み合わせることで、衝撃に極端に強い素材が完成しつつあります。多方面への適用が見込まれており、そのうちのひとつは惑星探査関連です。

Word-Exercise

次の単語の意味を下のa～eから選びましょう。

Part I

1. degrade [　]　2. erosion [　]　3. collapse [　]　4. layer [　]　5. coverage [　]

a. 層　b. 崩壊する　c. (適用)範囲　d. 浸食　e. 劣化させる

Part II

1. rigor [　]　2. reinforce [　]　3. hostile [　]　4. formulation [　]
5. tremendous [　]

a. 公式化　b. 好ましくない　c. 補強する　d. 厳しさ　e. すさまじい

Pre-Study

次は太陽系に属する惑星を太陽からの距離の順に表したものです。❶～❺に相当する名称を英語で書いてみましょう。

Unit 13 A Safer Mission to Mars

▶ 1st Watch

映像の Part I、II を観て、1と2の英文が内容と一致していれば T を、していなければ F を○で囲みましょう。また、3と4の英文が正しい内容を表すように破線部に入る適切な語（句）を a〜c から選びましょう。

Part I ▶

1. Scientists have acquired thorough knowledge of homogeneous gels to protect astronauts. [T / F]
2. The dust on the surface of Mars is so sharp that it may get into space suits easily. [T / F]
3. On the surface of Mars, space suits can be -------- due to sharp sand-like particles.
   a. advanced   b. degraded   c. developed
4. The functions of nano-particles in sunscreen and the materials that scientists were studying are very --------.
   a. simple   b. common   c. alike

Part II ▶▶

1. Scientists are carrying out experiments treating the suit textiles with nano-particle gels. [T / F]
2. Occasional micro-meteorite strikes can happen in the low Earth orbit environment. [T / F]
3. In the laboratory on Earth, they demonstrated that -------- between the suit materials and nano-particle gels.
   a. a synergy effect developed
   b. oxygen radicals exist
   c. the environment can change
4. Scientists will expose their materials to the tremendous rigors of harsh space to investigate --------.
   a. exactly when they could reach Mars
   b. how the materials can withstand them
   c. what problem will occur on the International Space Station

▶ 2nd Watch

映像をもう一度観て、下線部に入る語句を記入して英文を完成させましょう。

Part I　　　　　　　　　　　　　　　🎧 DL 50　💿 CD2-22

Norman Wagner, PhD (University of Delaware):
A mission to Mars. We really want to develop materials that will [1]_____
_____,
both on the way and when they're on the surface of the planetary surface. And these advanced nano-structure materials require science that we don't have yet. So, that drives a need for scientific understanding and how homogeneous gels can be created, and how we can control that through the processes of these materials.

　So [2]_____ to working on Mars. The Martian dust, because there isn't a lot of erosion, is extremely sharp. So, you have very sharp sand-like particles everywhere; they get, the dust gets in everything. And that dramatically degrades the soft goods, the habitats, the spacesuits. Science was all about nano-particle systems that form homogeneous gels, and [3]_____ of those gels, how their mechanical properties change.

　The example of the sunscreen is a great one, right, because you got a material and as it ages, the, the structure that was put into that to keep it, as a cream and a homogeneous material of a nice yield stress, starts to collapse and fall apart. And as you get a liquid layer and it separates, and now [4]_____
_____, you're also not necessarily getting the coverage of the nano-particles that are absorbing the UV. So, the particles in sunscreen are actually very similar to the particles that we were studying in our work. If you get the aging right, as we've shown, you can actually strengthen the material at a time.

Part II　　　　　　　　　　　　　　　🎧 DL 51　💿 CD2-23

Wagner: Think of it as a nano-composite, where we take the existing or best suit materials that we can make now in terms of textiles, and treat them with these nano-particle gels in such a way that they dramatically work synergistically to reinforce each other. And [5]_____
_____; we're demonstrating this on the International Space Station.

80

The low Earth orbit environment is actually a very hostile environment. There's ⁶_____.
There's also, because we're at the very top end of the atmosphere, there still are oxygen radicals which are very corrosive and reactive. And occasionally there are micro-meteorite strikes. The International Space Station is armored in many different ways to protect against that and this is a candidate material for doing that.

So we will deploy various types of, uh, formulation of our configurations that would be used in the outer part of the Martian spacesuit, to put that at the front end of the International Space Station, on a test station called 'MISSE,' which is a materials test station designed to ⁷_____. And then it will be brought back down to Earth for further diagnostics and study. And partly we just want to prove out that these materials can withstand the tremendous rigors of lower Earth orbit. Obviously, that's a different environment than that on Mars, but (we) can't test it on Mars ⁸_____.

Notes
l.9 **homogenous gels** 均一ゲル　*l.20* **yield stress** 降伏応力　*l.29* **synergistically** 相乗的に　*l.32* **low Earth orbit environment** 地球低軌道環境　*l.37* **oxygen radical** 酸素ラジカル　*l.39* **micro-meteorite** 微小隕石　*l.43* **MISSE** 材料曝露実験装置（Materials International Space Station Experiment の略）

♀Vocabulary Build-Up

次のA，Bの（　）に、与えられた文字で始まる共通の単語を文中から探して記入し、文を完成させましょう（語形は必要に応じて変化させること）。

1. A My home doctor prescribed non-habit-(**fo**   ) sleeping pills.
　B It is said that bad habits are easily (**fo**   ).

2. A (**Ab**   ) in my video game, I missed my train stop.
　B Many summer cosmetics use UV-(**ab**   ) materials.

3. A Some stationery items have been (**de**   ) for left-handers.
　B Having a clear idea is important in (**de**   ) a house.

Phrase-Exercise

次の英文の（　）に適切な語句を語群から選びましょう（語形は必要に応じて変化させること）。

1. The couple has tried everything to stop their marriage from (　　　　　　　).

2. There are many ways that viruses can (　　　　　　　) the body.

3. She advised me to install antivirus software to (　　　　　　　) unauthorized access.

get in	prove out	fall apart	protect against	bring back

Composition-Exercise

[　] の語句を使い、日本文の意味を表す英文を完成させましょう。

1. その日焼け止めに含まれる粒子は、必ずしも紫外線を吸収するものではありません。[necessarily]
   The particles in this sunscreen _____.

2. 両者が互いに補強しあうような形で、我々は2つの素材を処理するつもりです。[such]
   We're going to treat both materials in _____
   _____.

3. プロジェクト長はチームに、その問題を解決する方法があることを証明するように命令した。[prove]
   The project manager demanded the team to _____
   _____.

Unit 13 A Safer Mission to Mars

◉ Summarizing-Exercise   🎧 DL 52   💿 CD2-24

以下は映像の要約です。(　　　) に与えられた文字で始まる適語を入れて、文を完成させましょう。

> If we plan a mission to Mars on a manned spacecraft, we have to solve lots of (c　　　) beforehand. Among other things, it would be essential to create a super tough (s　　　), for instance, to protect the (a　　　) securely from extreme temperature and cosmic (d　　　), etc.
>
> Today, researchers are experimenting with various formulations of (g　　　) to apply to existing (t　　　) so that they work synergistically. They have passed (l　　　) tests and now scientists are making further investigations, using the MISSE unit on the International Space Station under more (h　　　) and rigorous space conditions. True, they are still in the Earth's orbit, and not on Mars, but we must make do with this until we get there.

◉ Stopover Dialogue   🎧 DL 53   💿 CD2-25

次は "Protective Clothing in the 21st Century" という衣類の展示を見たあとの男女の会話です。これを聞いて、以下の問題に答えましょう。

① 女性はどんな素材の衣類が気に入りましたか。

[　　　　　　　　　　　　　　　　　　　　　　　　　　　　]

② 男性が気に入った "multipurpose protective suits" は、どんなものから身体を保護しますか。

[　　　　　　　　　　　　　　　　　　　　　　　　　　　　]

③ ここで紹介された以外にどんな防護服があるかを調べ、その名称と機能をまとめましょう。

名称〔　　　　　　　〕　機能〔　　　　　　　　　　　　　〕
名称〔　　　　　　　〕　機能〔　　　　　　　　　　　　　〕

Unit 14 Birds Know How to Glide
鳥から学ぶムダなき究極の飛行術

ある種の鳥が上昇気流を巧みに利用した飛行をすることは広く知られています。しかし、その詳しいメカニズムには謎が多く、バイオミメティクスの一環として生物学と航空工学の研究者を中心に解明が進められています。近年、特に注目を集めているのは、羽ばたかずに長距離移動が可能な理由の解明です。鳥の特性に学び、飛行機の滑空時間が飛躍的に延びる日が来るかもしれません。

◉ Word-Exercise

次の単語の意味を下のa〜eから選びましょう。

Part I ▶
1. soar [　]　2. turbulence [　]　3. current [　]　4. migrate [　]　5. gust [　]

a. 突風　　b. 舞い上がる　　c. 乱気流　　d. 移動（渡り）をする　　e. 気流

Part II ▶▶
1. chaotic [　]　2. spiraling [　]　3. altitude [　]　4. strategy [　]
5. autonomous [　]

a. 渦巻き状の　　b. 無秩序な　　c. 戦略　　d. 自律的な　　e. 高度

◉ Pre-Study

次は上昇気流（thermal）がつくられる過程を示した図です。①〜③の各説明の（　）に入る語を指定された文字から始めて記入してみましょう。

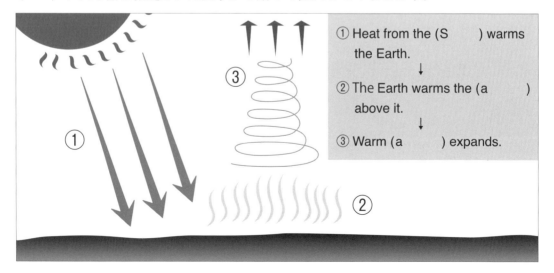

① Heat from the (S　　　) warms the Earth.
　↓
② The Earth warms the (a　　　) above it.
　↓
③ Warm (a　　　) expands.

Unit 14 Birds Know How to Glide

▶ 1st Watch

映像の Part I、II を観て、1と2の英文が内容と一致していればTを、していなければFを○で囲みましょう。また、3と4の英文が正しい内容を表すように破線部に入る適切な語（句）をa～cから選びましょう。

Part I ▶

1. For an energy-saving easy flight, birds must always seek out smooth air. [T / F]
2. When birds find hot pockets of air, they flap their wings much harder. [T / F]
3. Migrating birds must save energy so that they can continue to --------.
   a. avoid bumpy rides
   b. fly for many miles
   c. learn thermal soaring
4. Birds can use the rising air that they locate in order to -------- airborne.
   a. find
   b. save
   c. stay

Part II ▶▶

1. An untrained glider often spirals down out of control. [T / F]
2. Just like birds, a trained glider uses strong rising air currents. [T / F]
3. Provided with proper environmental cues, a trained glider will fly high even when they meet with -------- .
   a. better lift and soaring
   b. spiral patterns
   c. unstable air changes.
4. Human flying vehicles can learn a lot from our avian friends about how to --------.
   a. be more efficient, "go-with-the-flow" type of travelers
   b. gain altitude before bad weather strikes
   c. train autonomous gliders

85

▶ 2nd Watch

映像をもう一度観て、下線部に入る語句を記入して英文を完成させましょう。

Part I ▶   DL 54   CD2-26

Reporter: Hitting turbulence on a flight at 30,000 feet can cause quite the bumpy ride. But birds who soar high in the sky, not only handle bumpy air, [1]_____ a free, energy-saving lift. But how and why do they do that?

Ever watch a bird glide to the air effortlessly, rising higher and higher [2]_____? They do it by using a technique called thermal soaring. Birds can find hot, rising pockets of air and use the currents to stay aloft, and fly higher.

For birds who migrate thousands of miles, flapping their wings for long distances would require huge amounts of energy they don't have. So they use thermal soaring to [3]_____.

But the air currents are bumpy and turbulent, and exactly how birds use these wobbly gusts of air to stay airborne hasn't always been known.

Jerome Wong, PhD (University of California): This is one of the interesting parts with the birds, is that although the environment is extremely turbulent, so there are a lot of fluctuations in the, in the speed of the air, they are able to [4]_____.

Part II ▶   DL 55   CD2-27

Reporter: [5]_____ that learn to navigate these chaotic air environments, scientists at UC San Diego used math algorithms to train gliders to travel through complex, choppy air currents.

This graph shows how an untrained glider that [6]_____ will gradually fall, while a trained glider learns to use spiraling patterns in areas of strong rising currents, like in the thermal soaring of birds, and continues to gain altitude.

Scientists can train gliders to sense environmental cues, such as an increase in the twisting force of the wind, that indicate rising air. A trained glider uses the cues to stay within the thermal air current, and get better lift, leading to better soaring, even when there are strong, unstable air changes.

As changing air levels rise, the glider can gain height by using flight strategies it learned. One way to do this is to "go with the flow" of the turbulent rising air, [7]_____.

Wong: We have done some experiments where we have implemented it in a, in a real glider where we have put the algorithm, the policy, the strategy in the, in the glider. We put it up and we have clearly seen that the glider was able to gain height. We went from maybe 200 meters to more than six (hundred) quite easily in a few minutes.

Reporter: Learning how our avian friends use air currents could help autonomous gliders and other flying vehicles be [8]_____, which means the art of riding thermals isn't just "for the birds" anymore.

Notes
l.2 **bumpy ride** 揺れのひどい乗り心地　*l.16* **wobbly** 不安定な（choppy〈*l.25*〉は類似表現）
l.24 **algorithms** アルゴリズム（問題を解くための手順を定式化して表現したもの）　*l.38* **have implemented** 実行に移した

Vocabulary Build-Up

次のA, Bの（　）に、与えられた文字で始まる共通の単語を文中から探して記入し、文を完成させましょう（語形は必要に応じて変化させること）。

1. **A** This book is so old that we have to (**ha**　　　) it with extreme care.
   B Chronic stress could be a disaster if not (**ha**　　　) properly.

2. **A** No appointment is (**re**　　　) to attend the town hall meeting.
   B The development of software (**re**　　　) higher skills and knowledge.

3. **A** Look at the graph (**in**　　　) the percentage of female workers in our office.
   B As (**in**　　　) by the name, this spice originates from China.

Phrase-Exercise

次の英文の（　）に適切な語句を語群から選びましょう（語形は必要に応じて変化させること）。

1. The little boy is curious about how sound (　　　　　) the air.

2. The company created a drone that can (　　　　　) for a month at a time.

3. The car was hit by a bus as it was (　　　　　) the driveway.

glide through	stay aloft	travel through	go with	turn out of

Composition-Exercise

［　］の語句を使い、日本文の意味を表す英文を完成させましょう。

1. 渡り鳥がどのくらい高く飛べるのかは、正確には分かっていません。[migrating]
   Exactly _____
   is not known.

2. この飛行計画で、グライダーは不安定な天候でも飛翔が可能になります。[even]
   This flight plan allows a glider to soar _____
   _____.

3. いったん高度が上がれば、流れに逆らうよりはそれに身を任せる方がよい。
   [rather than]
   Once gaining height, you _____
   _____ against it.

Summarizing-Exercise

DL 56　CD2-28

以下は映像の要約です。（　　　）に与えられた文字で始まる適語を入れて、文を完成させましょう。

　　Birds will fly thousands of miles when they (**m**　　　). It would be hard labor and require tremendous energy if they had to flap their wings busily all the way. In fact, they use a smart technique called (**t**　　　) (**s**　　　). The idea is to catch and ride a rising air current so that they can stay (**a**　　　) effortlessly.

　　Now researchers have devised the math algorithm—the policy or strategy—for flying a model glider. As expected, the trained glider was able to (**s**　　　) environmental cues that suggest rising air, and successfully stay within such (**t**　　　) air currents. In (**s**　　　) patterns, the glider kept on soaring to higher (**a**　　　), imitating migrating birds.

Stopover Dialogue

DL 57　CD2-29

パラグライダーについて男女が話しています。この会話を聞いて、以下の問題に答えましょう。

① 女性はパラグライダーの現状をどう表現していますか。

［　　　　　　　　　　　　　　　　　　　　　　　　　　　　　］

② 男性は、なぜパラグライダーが高く飛んでも行方知れずになる心配はないと言っていますか。

［　　　　　　　　　　　　　　　　　　　　　　　　　　　　　］

③ パラグライダー以外に、風向きや気流を利用したスポーツを挙げてみましょう。

［　　　　　　　　　　　　　　　　　　　　　　　　　　　　　］

Unit 15 Better Biofuels from Corn
新局面を迎えたバイオ燃料開発

雄大なトウモロコシ畑はアメリカの典型的風景のひとつ。この豊富なトウモロコシを活かしたバイオ燃料開発で先端をいくアメリカが新たな手法による開発に乗り出しました。果皮と呼ばれる非食用部分を主に利用するこの手法は、燃料としての質の高さのみならず、食用と燃料用とでトウモロコシを奪い合う争いをなくすという利点も備えています。キーワードは「セルロース」です。

Word-Exercise

次の単語の意味を下のa～eから選びましょう。

Part I

1. quest [   ]   2. row [   ]   3. maize [   ]   4. starch [   ]   5. enzymes [   ]

a. 並び   b. でんぷん   c. 探求   d. トウモロコシ   e. 酵素

Part II

1. solution [   ]   2. ultrasound [   ]   3. obstacle [   ]   4. concern [   ]
5. diluted [   ]

a. 障害   b. 超音波   c. 薄められた   d. 懸念   e. 溶液

Pre-Study

次は再生可能エネルギーを紹介したものです。A～Eの（　　）に当てはまる単語を指定された文字から始めて記入してみましょう。

A. (g   ) energy
B. (w   ) energy
C. (h   ) energy
D. (s   ) energy
E. (b   ) energy

Unit 15 Better Biofuels from Corn

1st Watch

映像の Part I、II を観て、1と2の英文が内容と一致していればTを、していなければFを○で囲みましょう。また、3と4の英文が正しい内容を表すように破線部に入る適切な語（句）を a ～ c から選びましょう。

Part I

1. The air quality in large cities is hardly damaged by the thick smoke exhausted from cars and factories. [T / F]
2. We have already developed the types of plant-based fuel that are most cost-effective. [T / F]
3. Some researchers hope that biomass fuels, as -------- resources, will soon supply the industry with necessary energy.
   a. natural   **b.** renewable   **c.** unhealthy
4. The outer shell of the corn kernel is treated with enzymes and -------- starch and cellulose.
   a. digests   **b.** feeds   **c.** releases

Part II

1. The corn cellulose is fermented and becomes one of the enzymes. [T / F]
2. Biomass engineers are trying to make the cellulose solution flow well with other liquids. [T / F]
3. They are faced with -------- to overcome before producing ethanol more easily.
   a. fluids
   b. formulas
   c. obstacles
4. The process of diluting biomass fuels with lots of water and then taking out that water later --------.
   a. cannot move through pipes smoothly
   b. does not take much energy
   c. is not cost effective

91

▶ 2nd Watch

映像をもう一度観て、下線部に入る語句を記入して英文を完成させましょう。

Part I 🎧 DL 58 💿 CD2-30

Reporter: Smog is choking off air quality in large cities around the world. Thick smoke billows from factories. Cars clog highways and pump exhaust behind them. Scientists say [1]_____ _____ to unhealthy levels. Fossil fuels still power the industrial revolution but researchers hope renewable resources will soon power more of our planet, and save it. The quest for better biomass fuels takes us to America's heartland.

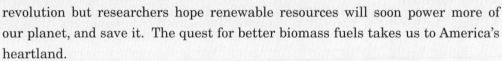

Corn is one of America's biggest cash crops. Huge fields fill America's heartland with rows of golden maize. We already use corn-based ethanol in our cars, but scientists want to create more cost-effective fuels [2]_____ _____. In labs across America, researchers are trying to engineer effective biomass fuels [3]_____.

Jason Bice is doing his part. He believes the best biofuels of tomorrow could come from the skin that covers a tiny corn kernel. That coating is called *pericarp* and it's a [4]_____.

Jason Bice (Purdue University): What pericarp is, is the shell of the corn kernel. They fractionate the corn first. It's milled. So the corn is already fractured into a lot of pieces, it's fractionated into starch, its oil and its pericarp's skin components. The pericarp is then separated out and then fed back through and they put enzymes into these batches of corn pericarp. And the enzymes, they digest the pericarp skin and they release from the pericarp starch and cellulose.

Part II 🎧 DL 59 💿 CD2-31

Reporter: That cellulose ferments and becomes a key component in ethanol. Researchers are working on ways to make that cellulose solution [5]_____ _____ so we can pump it through pipes and into our gas tanks.

Bice: As you introduce cellulose and hemicellulose and starches into the system from the enzymes digesting it, you create a more complex fluid that creates a lot of very interesting behavior.

Reporter: Biomass engineers are working to find the perfect flow rate using corn kernel skin, to make mass production of ethanol easier.

Bice: We're looking at characterizing that fluid with ultrasound speckle velocimetry. And so basically, that is the tool that uses ultrasound to image
6 _____ within a rheometer.

Reporter: Researchers have obstacles to overcome as they work on using corn kernel skins in renewable fuels. Cost is one concern. Right now, researchers can make diluted biomass fuels with lots of water and low salt concentrations, but
7 _____ .

Bice: It's not cost-effective because at the end they have to take out that water through reheating. That costs a lot of money, takes a lot of energy.

Reporter: Solving these problems will help scientists engineer renewable fuels that can compete with oil, gas and coal. It's important work to move tomorrow's ethanol industry from a tiny kernel of corn in the lab to an energy source that
8 _____ . This is Inside Science.

Notes

l.3 **billows** 渦を巻いて吹き出す　*l.3* **clog** 塞ぐ　*l.11* **cash crops** 市場用作物、換金作物　*l.16* **biofuels** 生物（バイオ）燃料　*l.18* **pericarp** 果皮　*l.20* **fractionate** （混合物を）分別する　*l.32* **hemicellulose** ヘミセルロース（植物中にセルロースと共に含まれる多糖類）　*l.37* **ultrasound speckle velocimetry** 超音波スペックル速度計　*l.39* **rheometer** 流量計

📍Vocabulary Build-Up

次のA, Bの（　）に、与えられた文字で始まる共通の単語を文中から探して記入し、文を完成させましょう（語形は必要に応じて変化させること）。

1. **A** When I visited Mongolia, I enjoyed some traditional (**fe**　　　) milk.
   B Sake is produced by (**fe**　　　) rice.

2. **A** A new autobiography of the famous musician was (**re**　　　) online.
   B Laughing is one of the most effective means of (**re**　　　) stress.

3. **A** She has not yet (**ov**　　　) her childhood fear of dark places.
   B There are several steps in (**ov**　　　) an unhealthy eating habit.

Phrase-Exercise

次の英文の（　）に適切な語句を語群から選びましょう（語形は必要に応じて変化させること）。

1. In a recycle center, all the plastic items are (　　　　　) tiny pieces every day.

2. Taxes on imported goods can (　　　　　) consumer spending.

3. (　　　　　) a small notebook from the bag, the painter started to draw a rough sketch.

```
   choke off    fracture into    work on    take out    compete with
```

Composition-Exercise

[　]の語句を使い、日本文の意味を表す英文を完成させましょう。

1. この国の増大するエネルギー需要を満たすため、彼らはコーンからバイオ燃料を作ろうとしている。[meet]
To _____,
they are trying to produce biofuels from corn.

2. 研究者たちはコスト効率面で化石燃料と競争できる手段を見つけようと取り組んでいます。[cost-effectively]
Researchers are working on ways to _____
_____.

3. バイオ燃料の大量生産をもっと容易にするために、この液体の流量を知ることが不可欠です。[mass]
_____,
it is essential to learn the fluid's flow rate.

Unit 15　Better Biofuels from Corn

Summarizing-Exercise

以下は映像の要約です。（　　　）に与えられた文字で始まる適語を入れて、文を完成させましょう。

Due to greenhouse gas emissions, the planet's air (p　　　) has been brought to unhealthy levels. Now we should stop relying on fossil fuels and search for some cleaner and (r　　　) energy sources. Scientists are trying to engineer more effective (b　　　) fuels, such as corn-based ethanol, as promising alternatives.

How is corn converted into a fuel? First, the shell of the corn kernel is (m　　　) and then (d　　　) by the working of enzymes and finally cellulose is (r　　　), which becomes a key component in ethanol. Researchers are trying hard to find the best flow rate for the cellulose (s　　　), which is a necessary step in producing ethanol cost-effectively. At present, the whole process costs a lot of money and takes a lot of energy. They need a better (f　　　) to meet the planet's demand for clean energy.

Stopover Dialogue

再生可能エネルギーについて男女が話しています。この会話を聞いて、以下の問題に答えましょう。

① 女性の考える再生可能エネルギーの1位と2位は何ですか。
1位〔　　　　　　　　　　　〕　2位〔　　　　　　　　　　　〕

② 女性がトウモロコシやサトウキビを燃料以外にとっておきたい理由は何ですか。
〔

〕

③ ペアを組んで、お互いが最適だと思う再生可能エネルギーとその理由を挙げてみましょう。
最適な再生可能エネルギー〔　　　　　　　　　　　　　　　　　　　〕
理由〔　　　　　　　　　　　　　　　　　　　　　　　　　　　　　〕

このテキストのメインページ
www.kinsei-do.co.jp/plusmedia/40

次のページのQRコードを読み取る直接ページにジャンプできます

オンライン映像配信サービス「plus⁺Media」について

本テキストの映像は plus⁺Media ページ（www.kinsei-do.co.jp/plusmedia）から、ストリーミング再生でご利用いただけます。手順は以下に従ってください。

ログイン

ログインページ

● ご利用には、ログインが必要です。
サイトのログインページ（www.kinsei-do.co.jp/plusmedia/login）へ行き、plus⁺Media パスワード（次のページのシールをはがしたあとに印字されている数字とアルファベット）を入力します。

● パスワードは各テキストにつき１つです。
有効期限は、はじめてログインした時点から１年間になります。

[利用方法]

次のページにある QR コード、もしくは plus⁺Media トップページ（www.kinsei-do.co.jp/plusmedia）から該当するテキストを選んで、そのテキストのメインページにジャンプしてください。

「Video」「Audio」をタッチすると、それぞれのメニューページにジャンプしますので、そこから該当する項目を選べば、ストリーミングが開始されます。

[推奨環境]

iOS (iPhone, iPad)	OS: iOS 6 ～ 12 ブラウザ：標準ブラウザ	Android	OS: Android 4.x ～ 8.0 ブラウザ：標準ブラウザ、Chrome
PC	OS: Windows 7/8/8.1/10, MacOS X	ブラウザ：Internet Explorer 10/11, Microsoft Edge, Firefox 48以降, Chrome 53以降, Safari	

※最新の推奨環境についてはウェブサイトをご確認ください。
※上記の推奨環境を満たしている場合でも、機種によってはご利用いただけない場合もあります。また、推奨環境は技術動向等により変更される場合があります。予めご了承ください。

本書には CD（別売）があります

Inside Science
映像で学ぶ 最新科学の深層

2019 年 1 月 20 日　初版第 1 刷発行
2025 年 2 月 20 日　初版第 9 刷発行

編著者　　野﨑嘉信
　　　　　松本和子
　　　　　Alastair Graham-Marr

発行者　　福岡正人
発行所　　株式会社　金星堂
（〒101-0051）東京都千代田区神田神保町 3-21
Tel. (03) 3263-3828（営業部）
　　(03) 3263-3997（編集部）
Fax (03) 3263-0716
https://www.kinsei-do.co.jp

編集担当　長島吉成　　　　　Printed in Japan
印刷所・製本所／三美印刷株式会社

本書の無断複製・複写は著作権法上での例外を除き禁じられています。本書を代行業者等の第三者に依頼してスキャンやデジタル化することは、たとえ個人や家庭内での利用であっても認められておりません。
落丁・乱丁本はお取り替えいたします。

ISBN978-4-7647-4077-8　C1082